Feminism within the Science and Health Care Professions: Overcoming Resistance

the ATHENE series

General Editors

**Gloria Bowles
Renate Klein
Janice Raymond**

Consulting Editor

Dale Spender

The ATHENE SERIES assumes that all those who are concerned with formulating explanations of the way the world works need to know and appreciate the significance of basic feminist principles.

The growth of feminist research has challenged almost all aspects of social organization in our culture. The ATHENE SERIES focuses on the construction of knowledge and the exclusion of women from the process — both as theorists and subjects of study — and offers innovative studies that challenge established theories and research.

ON ATHENE — When Metis, goddess of wisdom who presided over all knowledge was pregnant with ATHENE, she was swallowed up by Zeus who then gave birth to ATHENE from his head. The original ATHENE is thus the parthenogenetic daughter of a strong mother and as the feminist myth goes, at the "third birth" of ATHENE she stops being Zeus' obedient mouthpiece and returns to her real source: the science and wisdom of womankind.

Feminism within the Science and Health Care Professions: Overcoming Resistance

Edited by

SUE V. ROSSER

University of South Carolina, Columbia

PERGAMON PRESS

OXFORD · NEW YORK · BEIJING · FRANKFURT
SÃO PAULO · SYDNEY · TOKYO · TORONTO

U.K.	Pergamon Press, Headington Hill Hall, Oxford OX3 0BW, England
U.S.A.	Pergamon Press, Maxwell House, Fairview Park, Elmsford, New York 10523, U.S.A.
PEOPLE'S REPUBLIC OF CHINA	Pergamon Press, Room 4037, Qianmen Hotel, Beijing, People's Republic of China
FEDERAL REPUBLIC OF GERMANY	Pergamon Press, Hammerweg 6, D-6242 Kronberg, Federal Republic of Germany
BRAZIL	Pergamon Editora, Rua Eça de Queiros, 346, CEP 04011, Paraiso, São Paulo, Brazil
AUSTRALIA	Pergamon Press Australia, P.O. Box 544, Potts Point, N.S.W. 2011, Australia
JAPAN	Pergamon Press, 8th Floor, Matsuoka Central Building, 1-7-1 Nishishinjuku, Shinjuku-ku, Tokyo 160, Japan
CANADA	Pergamon Press Canada, Suite No. 271, 253 College Street, Toronto, Ontario, Canada M5T 1R5

First edition 1988

Library of Congress Cataloging in Publication Data
Rosser, Sue Vilhauer.
Feminism within the science and health care professions: overcoming resistance
Sue V. Rosser.
p. cm. — (The ATHENE series)
1. Science—Study and teaching. 2. Health education. 3. Women—
Study and teaching. 4. Curriculum planning. 5. Feminism.
I. Title. II. Series.
Q181.R683   1987   507'.1—dc 19   87–29205

British Library Cataloguing in Publication Data
Rosser, Sue V.
Feminism within the science and health
care professions: overcoming resistance. — (The
Athene series).
1. Women in science
I. Title II. Series 509   Q130

ISBN 0–08–035558–7 Hardcover
ISBN 0–08–035557–9 Flexicover

Printed in Great Britain by A. Wheaton & Co. Ltd., Exeter

In memory of
Ruth Bleier

Contents

Part 4 Conclusion

1
Introduction

Women in Science and Health Care: A Gender at Risk

Sue V. Rosser

Feminism within the Science and Health Care Profession: Overcoming Resistance has its roots on a session presented at the 1986 National Women's Studies Association Conference. Four of the chapter authors from this volume participated in that session. Since all of us had been dedicated feminists and scientists for at least 15 years we were troubled by our perception of a dream that had not been realized completely.

Each of us had observed the impact of feminism on various disciplines and professions of the humanities and social sciences as more women entered those fields during the 1970s. In subjects as diverse as history, anthropology, English, and psychology the feminist perspective had transformed some of the traditional theories and methodologies of the disciplines. We had naturally assumed that the sciences would be similarly transformation process. However, we thought that having a critical mass of and the nature of science itself would undoubtedly slow down the transformation process. However we thought that having a critical mass of women in science would eventually cause the change we were seeking.

Re-evaluating our assumptions in the mid-1980s made us eager to seek out more data about the feminist impact on the sciences. We suspected that resistances to feminism were arising at a variety of levels in the various professions within the science and health care establishment. Some were overt and might be classified as resistance to women's entrance into a field, advancement within the profession, or access to funding. Others were more subtle and might be considered as resistance to feminism — editorial policies favoring mainstream interpretations of data, lack of incorporation of feminist scholarship and issues into sessions at national meetings, or cooption and distorted presentation of feminist theories as mainstream science and health care ideas and policy. By exploring resistances to both women and feminism in a variety of disciplines within the sciences and

3

health care professions we hoped to be able to evaluate the impact and possibility for feminist transformations.

In order to begin to understand these resistances it is helpful to examine some of the forces of socialization and education which lead people to choose to study science and health care. The forces of socialization begin at birth and continue throughout an entire lifetime. The curriculum and methodological approaches used in the education system from preschool through graduate school tend to augment and reinforce the forces found in the family and larger society. Each educational or socialization incident may be minor. Taken by itself it might have little or no effect upon career choice or attitudes towards women and feminism. Added together with all of the other incidents it may be the final factor that steers many people, particularly women, away from the level of decision-making positions in science and health care. This in turn may lead to a science that resists feminist perspectives and theories and to individual men and women scientists and health care practitioners who are resistant to the contribution that feminist perspectives might make to science and health care. I would like to examine some of the factors, beginning at birth and extending throughout our educational and professional lives, that may lead scientists and health care practitioners to resist women and feminism within the professions.

For example, we know from the studies of Rubin et al. (1974) that baby boys and baby girls are treated very differently, beginning at birth. What is the first question that most people ask as soon as the baby is born? Is it a boy or girl? Based on the answer to that question, people begin to respond differently to the newborn. Rubin et al. (1974) interviewed 30 first-time parents, 15 of girls and 15 of boys, within 24 hours of the baby's birth. The parents of girls rated their babies softer, more finely featured, smaller, and more inattentive than did the parents of boys. Fathers seemed especially influenced by the gender of the child and described their sons as firmer, larger-featured, better coordinated, more alert, stronger, and hardier than did the mothers. Men thought their daughters were more inattentive, weak, and delicate than the women did. There was only one exception. Mothers rated sons cuddlier than daughters, and fathers rated daughters cuddlier than sons. But hospital personnel had routinely examined each baby after birth for physical and neurological characteristics such as color, muscle tone, reflex irritability and matched them so that there were *no* differences between males and females, even in size. Sex-role stereotyping and perceptions of differences between males and females begin immediately.

This differential treatment continues, despite the perception of the parents that they are treating their male and female children equally. Will and his colleagues (1974) set up an experiment in which they dressed a six-month-old child in neutral-colored clothing. Eleven mothers were observed to see which of the three toys, a train, a doll, or a fish they would offer the child. Those women who were told that the baby was a girl offered the doll more frequently than the train; those who were told that the baby was a boy, offered the train more frequently than the doll. Afterwards two mothers commented that "Beth" was a real girl, because she was sweeter and cried more softly than a boy could. In fact "Beth" was a boy. A really notable feature of this study is that all of the women claimed to believe that males and females are alike at this tender age, and none said that she would treat her own sons and daughters differently. On the contrary nine of the eleven insisted that they encouraged rough play with their daughters, and ten said that they encouraged their sons to play with dolls.

Lynn (1966, 1969) and Chodorow (1978) suggest that parents encourage boys to separate from their mothers and become "autonomous and independent" while girls are discouraged from separating. The experiments testing these theories (Maccoby and Jacklin 1974) are somewhat contradictory but the data tend to support the idea that boys are encouraged to be more independent and aggressive. Certainly boys and girls are subjected to different sex-role socialization processes from parents, the media, and institutions in the surrounding society and exhibit some developmental differences during the preschool period.

By the time children reach elementary school, girls are more mature than boys, are ready for verbal and math skills at an earlier age, and have better control of small-motor skills. As Shakeshaft (1986) has pointed out, however, the curriculum, disciplinary system, and environment are all based upon male models of development. Thus the grades (or ages) at which various mathematics and verbal skills are introduced fit male needs rather than those of females. The absence of women from most subjects in the curriculum leaves many girls feeling alienated and makes it more difficult for them to see the material as relating to them. The co-educational environment, found in virtually all public schools, favors boys because boys behave better when girls are present. In contrast girls learn better, show higher self-esteem, and receive more leadership opportunities in single-sex environments.

The work of Sadker and Sadker (1986) documents the fact that boys receive more attention from teachers than girls in co-educational environments. They found that boys in elementary school are eight times as likely as girls to call out and demand attention. Their demands are rewarded, since teachers accept the answers from boys. But when girls exhibited this same behavior teachers corrected them, telling them to raise their hands. Thus the tendency towards aggressive behavior that may have been encouraged by the preschool boy's parents is reinforced in the elementary school environment by the teacher.

The teacher especially may be a crucial figure in helping to develop differential attitudes and skills towards science and mathematics in elementary school-aged boys and girls. Most elementary school teachers are women. The traditional training for elementary school teachers requires minimal competency in basic science and mathematics. This minimal training coupled with the women's own sex-role socialization produces many elementary school teachers who themselves do not feel comfortable with science. Some are very blatant, as was my daughter's first grade teacher, who stated that she did not like science and did not teach it. She said that she believed in concentrating on the basics, which she defined as reading, writing, and arithmetic. Obviously this teacher represents an extreme which conveys a negative impression of science to both boys and girls. I hope her example is not present in most classrooms throughout the country. However, even blatant behavior such as hers may differentially affect boys and girls. A boy who likes science recognizes that his teacher is female and can more easily choose not to identify with her attitudes towards science which he may view as a female feeling about the subject. But a girl who likes science may find it more difficult not to accept the attitude towards science of a teacher with whom she identifies in other respects.

Even when elementary schools are trying to teach science, and use hands-on experiences involving both boys and girls, the teaching methods and subtleties in the way the material is presented may result in a different learning experience for boys and girls in the same classroom. For example, many elementary teachers ask the students to "build a terrarium" to introduce concepts related to ecology, micro-environments, and oxygen supplies. Although the entire class participates in the project, all too frequently the boys go out to gather the soil, plants and animals, while the girls remain inside to "decorate the terrarium" (Gazzam-Johnson 1985). Aside from the reinforcement of male-active and female-passive sex role stereotypes which this exercise promotes, the boys have learned much more about field work and plant and animal habitats than have the girls.

A similar lack of learning and reinforcement of passive roles for girls occurs when the teachers do the experiment, solve the math problem, or answer the question for little girls. Research has indicated that these teachers are more likely to provide different feedback for boys who give wrong answers. Boys are told to try harder, while girls are praised for simply trying (Stallings 1980). Data from the 1976–77 NAEP (National Assessment of Educational Progress) indicate that although nine-year-old girls have significantly less experience with scientific observations and the use of science instruments than nine-year-old boys (Kahle and Lakes 1983), the girls *desire* to have such experiences. It is particularly unfortunate that our elementary schools are not providing them with the experiences.

By junior high the girls have lost much of their desire to participate in scientific activities (Kahle and Lakes 1983). In addition thirteen-year-old girls have fewer science experiences than boys compared with nine-year-old girls; the disparity in science experiences between boys and girls increases with age. Not too surprisingly this decline parallels a decline in science achievement levels also (Matyas 1985). Although the girls' scores in mathematics achievement decline in junior high school, approximately half of the few sex differences found in mathematics do favor girls at that age (Campbell 1986).

Junior high school corresponds with the age when girls are reaching puberty. Numerous studies have indicated that puberty is the time when sex role expectations become more rigidly enforced. Parents buy their sons more science- and math-related toys and computers than they buy their daughters (Campbell 1986). They also have higher expectations of achievement in math and more strongly encourage their sons to take math courses. Boys are also urged to enroll in after-school and outside-of-school science and technology programs (Campbell 1984). Teachers may also convey in direct and more subtle ways their differing expectations for boys and girls. For example, in the summer of 1985 a math teacher "assigned a boy who spoke very little English the task of correcting the girls' classwork, while she corrected the boys' work and gave them individual feedback." (Campbell 1986, p. 517). Guidance counselors may routinely discourage girls from the science and math track because they assume that high verbal scores mean they are a "reading and writing" person. (Campbell 1986). Unfortunately, many guidance counselors reflect their own attitudes regarding traditional careers for men and women in their counseling of students (Remick and Miller 1978). Girls are not counseled to take the mathematics courses and provided with information on the higher-paying careers which are seen as traditionally male.

By high school the subtle and not-so-subtle long-term effects of parents, teachers, counselors, and peers become evident. Girls have fewer science experiences with instruments and materials and score lower on science and mathematical achievement tests than boys.

Throughout high school girls take fewer mathematics courses than boys. Girls also have higher attrition rates than boys from these classes. These higher attrition rates are not due to poor grades, because girls have higher grades in mathematics classes (Remick and Miller 1978) than boys. Girls choosing to continue science and mathematics during high school may be viewed as nonconformists at a developmental period when conformity is highly valued by peers. "Girls taking science courses describe themselves as '. . .less feminine, less attractive, less popular, and less sociable. That is, they appear to see themselves as less socially attractive than their peers' " (Smithers and Collins in Kelly 1981, p. 166). Fox (in Iker 1980) states that many girls do not enter accelerated math courses because of negative social consequences, especially peer rejection. Since science and math are not seen as part of the female sex role, girls in coeducational classes feel particular pressure not to choose those subjects. (Omerod 1975).

The curriculum content often reflects little of women's experiences or theories that are relevant to girl's lives. Although this is a major difficulty in the content of all disciplines (McIntosh 1983), it is a particularly severe problem in the sciences (Rosser 1986). Contributions of women to science must be portrayed seriously in narrative as well as illustrative materials. "The inclusion of women photographed in lab coats was inadequate; their real contributions must be discussed. Our studies suggested that if the repeated message from teacher and text was that scientists were males, adolescent girls, unsure of their feminity would shy away from science or, if enrolled, would perform poorly" (Kahle 1985, p. 197).

The attrition rates coupled with fewer girls enrolling in mathematics courses result in girls entering college with, on the average, one-third less high school mathematics than boys (NSF, 1982; Chipman and Thomas, 1980). A further result is girls scoring lower on the mathematics section of achievement tests for college. Some tests, such as the SAT, upon which girls score almost fifty points lower than boys (449 vs. 495 in 1984), show more sex-related differences than others such as the ACT (Campbell 1986).

Since high school mathematics is a requirement for many occupations and fields of study, mathematics is often called the "critical filter" in the training of future scientists and engineers. Researchers estimate that high school graduates with less than four years of high school mathematics may be filtered out of three-fourths of all college majors (Tobin in Iker 1980). These majors are usually the ones leading to the higher-paying jobs. Thus girls become the "gender at risk." As Sadker and Sadker (1986) so succinctly sum up the effect of elementary and secondary school on girls: "What other group starts out ahead — in reading, in writing, and even in math — and 12 years later finds itself behind?"

Using case studies of teachers, Kahle has pinpointed teaching behaviors and techniques effective for retaining women in science.

TABLE 0.1. *Teaching Behaviors and Techniques Effective for Retaining Women in Science*

DO	DON'T
use laboratory and discussion activities	use sexist humor
provide career information	use sex-stereotyped examples
directly involve girls in science activities	distribute sexist classroom materials
provide informal academic counseling	allow boys to dominate discussions or
demonstrate unisex treatment in science	activities
classrooms	allow girls to resist passively

"These ten special teaching behaviors and instructional strategies resulted in proportionately more girls in their classes continuing in math and science courses in both high school and college" (Kahle 1985, p. 74). Few teachers seem to be following these behaviors.

In college the situation for women students does not improve. Studies have demonstrated that throughout the college years women in all majors tend to show a gradual decline in self-esteem. (Astin 1977). Neither male nor female students who have not passed the critical filter of four years of high school mathematics are likely to switch to major in science, math, or a technological field while in college. During the college years the potential pool of scientists becomes smaller rather than larger. The women students who did pass the mathematics critical filter, however, drop out in larger percentages than the men students do. In their report "The Classroom climate: A Chilly One for Women?" Hall and Sandler (1982) point out the factors in student-student and student-teacher interactions which lead to difficulties and lowered self-esteem for all women students. They underline the particular difficulties for women majoring in traditionally masculine fields such as science:

- they comprise a distinct minority in a given class or department;
- they have little contact with other women pursuing the same major because of the vertical progression of required courses;
- they find few female teachers who might serve as role models; and
- they work with many professors who are not accustomed to having women students in their classes. (p. 12).

Hall and Sandler (1982) report that a further deterrent to women staying in science is their own concern over the appropriateness of a "non-traditional" major. This concern echoes the situation in high school and was voiced again in the study by Baker (1983) which found that both male and female college students held the attitude that women majoring in science were less feminine than women majoring in non-science.

The 1986 NSF *Report on Women and Minorities in Science and Engineering* statistics show 38% of all science and engineering undergraduate degrees being awarded to women, despite the fact that women are earning more than half of the baccalaureate degrees now. These data include some fields such as psychology, traditionally considered to be a social science. The social sciences account for 53% of the degrees awarded to women. When life sciences are excluded from the data, the percentage of women is reduced even further. From 1973–1984, 27.6% of bachelor's degrees were awarded to women in the physical and mathematical sciences. Only 13% of undergraduate degrees in engineering are awarded to women.

The conflict between perception of lack of femininity and major in science was observed to increase at the graduate level, since many women stated the "fear of not being feminine" as a primary reason for not pursuing study in a scientific field. Furthermore the Graduate Record Examination (GRE) scores of women and men are about the same on the verbal component, but men score substantially higher on the quantitative component and slightly higher on the analytical component (NSF, 1986). Those few women who do undertake graduate study usually face more obstacles and receive less support than women in science at the undergraduate level. Sandler and Hall (1986) found that graduate women in science typically faced the following sorts of behaviors:

- Male students and faculty may indirectly or directly disparage women's abilities. ("Everyone knows women are not good in spatial ability.")
- Misperceptions based on stereotypes may be prevalent, such as expecting women in medicine to be more "caring," and steering them to those areas of medicine where "caring" is perceived as being more important (as in pediatrics).
- Faculty may be less willing to work with women students because they see women as having less potential and/or because they may be uncomfortable with women.
- Male peers may intentionally disrupt women's work, as in the case of a woman whose laboratory equipment was repeatedly decalibrated.
- Many students, especially those in engineering, math, economics, and science, report difficulties with foreign male students and faculty who come from cultures where women's role is very circumscribed. They often engage in numerous overt discriminatory behaviors such as sexual harassment, not calling on women students at all, not answering their questions, and openly ridiculing or disparaging women. Students complaining about such treatment often receive no support but are told instead to be "understanding" because that person comes from another culture (Sandler and Hall 1986, p. 17).

Other research has documented more subtle behaviors which may superficially appear egalitarian or even helpful to a woman scientist's career goal but which may in fact hurt her career in the long run. The classic example of this type of behavior is the practice of awarding more teaching assistantships to female graduate students, and more research assistantships to male graduate students, as Vetter documents in "Where Are the Women in the Physical Sciences?" The women usually like the interaction with students and often request the teaching assistantships. However enjoyable and useful for departmental purposes teaching may be, the current structure of science and career advancement reward research. The male graduate student who has a research assistantship can frequently make use of some if not all of his research data for his own dissertation. At a minimum he will learn to use procedures, equipment, and methods of analysis that will aid him in his dissertation. Furthermore, his assistantship will probably put him in contact with a network of individuals in the laboratory and in the wider scientific community who can serve as sources of information about methods, grants, and even employment opportunities. Although it is not impossible for the female teaching assistant to gather data, learn procedures, and develop a network, she must do so in addition to, rather than as a part of, her teaching responsibilities.

The teaching assistantship serves as an example of one of the many factors which may lead to a higher drop-out rate for female compared to male graduate students in science. The data from the 1986 *Report on Women and Minorities in Science and Engineering* demonstrate that 25% of the Ph.D.s in science and engineering are awarded to women. Of those, 41% (2,400) are in the social sciences; only 5% (150) are in engineering. The National Research Council Doctorate Research File records that the percent of all physical science and math doctorates awarded to women in the 1980s is 13.8%.

Since scarcity often leads to higher prices one might assume that the starting salaries for women scientists might be higher than those for men scientists. With one exception (engineering) this is not the case. In all scientific fields at all degree levels, women receive lower starting salaries than men with the same degrees (NSF 1986).

The situation for women scientists does not improve with increased time on the job. The NSF *Report on Women and Minorities in Science and Engineering* documents that women scientists have lower salaries, (71% of those for men in 1984) less chance for advancement, and higher unemployment than men scientists (more than twice that of men) in all fields and in all sectors (including government, industry, and academia.) The disparities increase with advancing rank. The individuals who prepared this report for the National Science Foundation (1986) applied a series of sophisticated statistical techniques to these data to equalize factors such as length of years of uninterrupted employment from the work force and previous post-doctoral experience. (It is often argued that women have lower rank and salary because they drop out to have children. Similarly some individuals have argued that higher rank and salary for male scientists reflect the higher percentage of male Ph.D.s who have additional years of post-doctoral training.) Even after such factors that might be biasing the data are controlled, much of the disparity could be accounted for by discrimination.

What are the results of a process, then, that begins at birth, actively and passively discouraging girls and women at every step of the way from entering fields in science and technology? One obvious result of the process is that we still have very few women in most fields. Betty Vetter's chapter documents the small number of women in the physical sciences.

Although the percentage of women in physical science has increased from 3.7% of the total in the 1950s to as much as 13.8% in the 1980–85 period the actual numbers are still very small.

Even when the numbers of women entering disciplines has become substantial the distribution of women within the subdisciplines or specialties within those fields may be skewed. Jennie Kronenfeld found this to be the case in her chapter, "Women in Public Health: Changes in a Profession." Joan Altekruse and Suzanne McDermott in "Contemporary Concerns of Women in Medicine" document that despite the fact that women are now residents in all subspecialties (except vascular surgery) high percentages are still practicing in "conventional" fields (internal medicine, pediatrics, and obstetrics/gynecology).

Another significant result is the effect that this process has on science itself. This process results in very few women reaching top-level and decision-making positions within the scientific hierarchy. The figures for academia show only about 4–6% of full professors being women. These figures would be even smaller if teaching institutions were excluded and the focus was on major research universities. In research universities only 5% of tenured faculty are women. For example, in 1983, in the chemistry departments in the U.S. that grant doctorates, women held only 4.1% of the faculty positions although they had earned 9.5% of all doctorates awarded by these universities in the last 20 years and 14% of those awarded during the last decade (Vetter and Babco 1986). The prestigious National Academy of Sciences has only 57 females out of 2,610 members elected since it was chartered in 1863 (Rubin 1986). On the NIH review panels the percentage of women members increased from 16.9% to 17.9% between 1975 and 1984. The total number of members almost doubled from 733 to 1264 in that time (Filner 1986).

Even the field of public health, historically a stronghold for women, has relatively few women at the top. In "Women in Public Health: Changes in a Profession" Jennie Kronenfeld documents the small numbers of women in faculty and state health officer positions, despite increasing numbers of women in the profession.

Because there are so few women in top-level and decision-making positions in science, historians and philosophers of science (Keller 1982; Hein 1981; Fee 1981, 1982) have described science as a masculine province which excludes women. Keller (1982) has described the four levels at which women are excluded or exclude ourselves from science.

1. Unfair employment practices that prevent women from reaching the theoretical and decision-making level of science.
2. Androcentric bias in the choice and definition of problems studied so that subjects concerning women, such as menstrual cramps, childbirth, and menopause, receive less funding and study.

3. Androcentric bias in the design and interpretation of experiments so that only male rats or monkeys are used as experimental subjects.
4. Androcentric bias in the formulation of scientific theories and methods so that unicausal, hierarchical theories that coincide with the male experience of the world become the "objective" theories that define the interpretation of the scientific data.

Joan Gero's chapter, "Gender Bias in Archeology: Here, Then, and Now" provides statistical data from the National Science Foundation that demonstrate less funding for women to do fieldwork than laboratory work. This has the effect of pushing more women into the laboratory (and more men into the field) and less funding and status for laboratory work. Altekruse and McDermott suggest that with more women physicians it is hopeful that more attention and study will be given to diseases of women.

Quite naturally the androcentric bias in the choice and definition of problems studied has led to androcentric bias and resistance to feminist theories and methods in science. Editorial policies which restrict the publication of data or comments that run counter to traditional scientific theories are explored by Ruth Bleier in "*Science* and the Construction of Meanings in the Neurosciences." She emphasizes the role of these policies in preventing the scientific community from becoming aware of data and approaches that are critical of androcentric theories. In the chapter "The Impact of Feminism on the AAAS Meetings: From Nonexistent to Negligible," I examine the extent to which feminist theories and issues are under-represented at the major national scientific meeting.

Due to the effects of editorial policy and structure of scientific meetings, and the active exclusion of women from science, both women and feminism are largely absent from this masculine science and health care system which has evolved. Because of the small number of women in theoretical and decision-making levels of science and health care the subjects explored, experimental models used, and theories formulated have largely excluded women. For these same reasons scientists and health care practitioners tend to resist feminist theories and critiques of traditional practice. Even some women scientists are resistant to the feminist critique that questions the objectivity of science.

At the same time that many scientists and health care practitioners have resisted feminism most feminists have resisted traditional science and health care. One clear reason for this resistance of feminists comes from their observation that few women have made the decisions and developed the theory of the science and health care systems, which they therefore view as masculine, patriarchal approaches to the world and women. Another reason that feminists may be resistant is that they have seen examples in traditional science and health care practice of take-over and distortion of feminist ideals into the mainstream.

In "The Response of the Health Care System to the Women's Health Movement," Nancy Worcester and Mariamne Whatley explore the methods by which the mainstream health care system has coopted popular ideas of the women's health movement. Mariamne Whatley suggests more creative, supportive methods by which feminist health theories and practices might be incorporated in "Beyond Compliance: Towards a Feminist Health Education."

The resistance barriers must be lowered on both sides. Scientists and health care practitioners must accept women in decision-making positions in the profession and be accepting of the feminist critique of the theories, methodologies, experimental subjects, and data interpretation. Feminists must accept science and health care as important realities in our technological society. Avoidance and mutual exclusion is likely to be harmful to both groups. The purpose of this volume is to explore the forms of resistances and the reasons for those resistances with the hope that understanding will lead to a lowering of barriers.

REFERENCES

Astin, A. 1977. *Four Critical Years: Effects of College on Beliefs, Attitudes, and Knowledge.* San Francisco: Jossey-Bass.

Baker, D. 1983. Can the difference between male and female science majors account for the low number of women at the doctoral level in science? *Journal of College Science Teaching,* Nov., 102–107.

Campbell, P. 1984. The Computer Revolution: Guess Who's Left Out? *Interracial Books for Children Bulletin,* **15**, 3–6.

Campbell, P. B. 1986. What's a Nice Girl Like You Doing in a Math Class? *Phi Delta Kappan,* March, 516–520.

Chipman, S. F., and Thomas, V. G. 1980. *Women's Participation in Mathematics: Outlining the Problem.* Washington, DC, Report to the National Institute of Education, Teaching, and Learning Division.

Chodorow, N. 1978. *The Reproduction of Mothering,* Berkeley, California, University of California Press.

Fee, E. 1981. Is feminism a threat to scientific objectivity? *International Journal of Women's Studies,* **4**, No. 4, 213–233.

Fee, E. 1982. A feminist critique of scientific objectivity. *Science for the People,* **14**, No. 4:8.

Filner, B. 1982. President's Remarks. *AWIS,* Vol. XV, No. 4, July/August.

Gazzam-Johnson, V. 1985. Personal communication.

Hall, R., and Sandler, B. 1982. *The Classroom Climate: A Chilly One for Women.* Washington, D.C.: Project on the Status and Education of Women, AAC.

Hein, H. 1981. Women and Science: Fitting Men to Think About Nature. *International Journal of Women's Studies,* **4**, 396–397.

Iker, S. 1980. A Math Answer for Women. *MOSAIC,* **11**, 39–45.

Kahle, J. B. 1985. *Women in Science.* Philadelphia: Falmer Press.

Kahle, J. B., and Lakes, M. K. 1983. The myth of equality in science classrooms. *Journal of Research in Science Teaching,* **20**, 131–140.

Keller, E. 1982. Feminism and science. *Signs: Journal of Women in Culture and Society,* **7**, No. 3, 589–602.

Kelly, A. 1981. *The Missing Half.* Manchester, England: Manchester University Press.

Lynn, D. 1966. The process of learning parental and sex-role identification. *Journal of Marriage and the Family*, **28**, 466–70.

Lynn, D. 1969. *Parental and Sex-role Identification: A Theoretical Formulation*. Berkeley, California: McCutchan.

Maccoby, E., and Jacklin, C. 1974. *The Psychology of Sex Differences*. Stanford, California: Stanford University Press.

Matyas, M. L. 1985. Obstacles and constraints on women in science. *Women in Science*, ed. J. B. Kahle, Philadelphia: Falmer Press.

McIntosh, P. 1983. Interactive phases of curricular revision: A feminist perspective. Working Paper No. 124, Wellesley College, Center for Research on Women, Wellesley, Mass.

National Science Foundation. 1986. *Report on Women and Minorities in Science and Engineering*, Washington, D.C.: NSF.

National Science Foundation. 1982. *Science and Engineering Education: Data and Information*. (NSF82–30). Washington, D.C.: NSF.

Ormerod, M. B. 1975. Subject preference and choice in coeducational and single-sex secondary schools. *British Journal of Educational Psychology*, **45**, 257–67.

Remick, H., and Miller, K. 1978. Participation rates in high school mathematics and science courses. *The Physics Teacher*, May, 280–282.

Rosser, S. 1986. *Teaching Science and Health from a Feminist Perspective: A Practical Guide*. New York: Pergamon Press.

Rubin, Z., Provenzano, J., and Luria, Z. 1974. The eye of the beholder: parents views on sex and newborns. *American Journal of Orthopsychiatry*, **44**, 512–19.

Rubin, V. 1986. Women's Work: For Women in Science, a Fair Shake is Still Elusive. *Science*, **86**, July/August, 58–65.

Sadker, M., and Sadker, Z. 1986. Sexism in the Classroom: From Grade School to Graduate School. *Phi Delta Kappan*, March, 512–515.

Sandler, B., and Hall, R. 1986. *The Campus Climate Revisited: Chilly for Women Faculty, Administrators, and Graduate Students*. Washington, D.C.: Project on the Status and Education of Women, AAC.

Shakeshaft, C. 1986. A Gender at Risk. *Phi Delta Kappan*, March, 499–503.

Stallings, J. 1980. Comparisons of Men's and Women's Behaviors in High School Math Classes. Washington, D.C.: National Institute of Education.

Vetter, B., and Babco, E. 1986. *Professional Women and Minorities: A Manpower Data Resource Service*, Sixth Edition. Washington, D.C.: Commission on Professionals in Science and Technology.

Will, C., Self, P., and Datan, N. 1974. Unpublished paper presented at 82nd annual meeting of the American Psychological Association.

2
Status in the Professions: Resistances to Women

Chapter 1

Where are the Women in the Physical Sciences?

Betty M. Vetter

Where are the women in the physical sciences and why are there so few of them after two decades of affirmative action? Although they have consistently been less well represented in these fields than in the life sciences far more women have earned degrees in the physical sciences than is indicated in the labor force data for these professions. Women earned 158,000 bachelor's degrees in the physical and environmental sciences in the period from 1950 to 1985. But less than a third of that number are reported still in the science labor force for those fields in 1986, compared with more than half of the number of men who earned similar bachelor's degrees during those years (Vetter and Babco 1987). The small difference between men and women in labor force participation does not explain the discrepancy. Thus in addition to the smaller numbers of women who have chosen these fields at the baccalaureate level there has been extensive loss attributable to other causes.

A little background is helpful in understanding what some of those causes may be, before examining the place of women today in the physical and mathematical sciences, including both their access to education and their opportunities for entrance and advancement in the professional workforce.

EDUCATION

Women's colleges were the major source of science baccalaureate education for women in the late nineteenth century, although some private and public universities also admitted women, both as undergraduates and as graduate students (Rossiter 1982). One of the first U.S. women to receive recognition in science was astronomer Maria Mitchell, who had learned from her father how to use a telescope to scan the sky, and how to calculate orbits. As a librarian at the Nantucket Athenaeum she studied

19

the advanced astronomical and mathematical texts available to her. In 1847, when only 29, she discovered a comet, earning a gold medal from the King of Denmark and becoming in the U.S. a symbol of women's entry into science. In 1848 she became the first woman elected into the American Academy of Arts and Sciences — the only woman so honored for the next 95 years. She was active in the American Association for the Advancement of Science and ultimately became the director of Vassar's new college observatory, opened in 1865 (Rubin 1986).

Astronomy was an attractive field for many women. By 1871, 18 of the women's academies had observatories and offered a course in astronomy. When the American Astronomical Society was founded in the 1890s the charter membership included eleven women, about 10% of all the charter members. By the beginning of the twentieth century significant numbers of women were employed in U.S. observatories, serving as human computers to do calculations and make measurements of photographic plates — work for which they were believed to be peculiarly suited. Between 1877 and 1919 the Harvard College observatory hired 45 women for these tasks, including Annie Jump Cannon, who was later awarded the first honorary degree ever bestowed on a woman by Oxford University (Rubin 1986).

In 1925 Cecilia Payne-Gasposchkin received the first Harvard Ph.D. in astronomy ever awarded. During the decade of the 1920s women earned almost 27% of all astronomy doctorates awarded by U.S. universities — the highest proportion of any science field (NRC 1973) (Table 1).

But the proportion of Ph.D.s in astronomy that were awarded to women dropped steadily through the next three decades, as it did in all science fields. Then, as now, women's representation in the physical sciences remained far below that in the social and life sciences.

With the advent of affirmative action and an open-door policy for women students at most academic institutions both the number and proportion of women started up again. In astronomy, however, that proportion even in 1985 is only about half as much as in the 1920s. It is not surprising, then, to find that almost a century after its founding the

TABLE 1.1. *Percent of Physical Science Doctorates Awarded to Women, by Decade*

	1920s	1930s	1940s	1950s	1960s	1970s	1980s*
Math and Computer Sciences	14.5	14.8	10.7	5.0	5.7	10.1	13.8
Astronomy	26.8	12.4	25.3	8.9	6.5	8.6	14.5
Physics	3.2	3.2	2.9	1.8	1.9	3.9	6.3
Chemistry	7.3	6.4	4.2	4.4	6.4	10.4	17.1
All Phys/Sci/Math Fields	7.6	6.6	5.0	3.7	4.6	8.2	13.8

*1980 through 1985
Data Source: National Research Council Doctorate Records File

American Astronomical Society membership today includes only about 300 women in its total membership of 4,000 — about 7% (Rubin 1986).

Astronomy is among the smallest of the physical science fields and its early attraction for women was not sustained. In part this may be related to the small number of job opportunities in the field. It may also reflect the many years in which women were not allowed to do research in U.S. observatories since use of the big telescopes was generally reserved for men.

Chemistry, the largest of the physical sciences, also has a long history of women participants. As early as 1922 the U.S. Bureau of Vocational Information published a report entitled "Women in Chemistry, A Study of Professional Opportunities," prepared by a committee of sixteen women chemists appointed by the American Association of University Women, who used information obtained by survey responses from 660 women chemists (American Chemical Society 1986). The report's appendix lists 34 universities that would admit women to a doctoral program in chemistry. During that decade women earned 7.3% of all the Ph.D. awards in this field (NRC 1973).

The American Chemical Society (ACS) had about 250 women members in 1921, in a total membership of 15,000 (1.7%). In 1976 ACS published the first of its series of special reports on women in chemistry, examining "The Economic Status of Women in the ACS." At that time women were 7.8% of ACS membership. "Women Chemists 1980," published in 1981, found that women were now 10% of U.S. members under age 65, who were neither emeritus nor student members. The most recent survey, in 1985, found that women make up 14.5% of ACS membership (ACS 1986).

These increasing proportions follow a similar pattern to doctoral awards in chemistry (Table 1). But as with astronomy, chemistry and the remaining physical sciences groups have retained their relative position among the science groups as the least likely to attract women.

Physics included only 3% women among its doctoral graduates in the 1920s. Although the proportion rose to 6% in the 1980s after the decreases through the 1950s (Table 1) the numbers have remained small. The proportion of women members in the affiliated societies of the American Institute of Physics is about 6% (American Institute of Physics 1986).

The geosciences were inhospitable to women long after the life sciences had opened up. Whether geology field trips were thought to be too strenuous for women students, or whether the thought of an overnight field trip with both men and women was considered prohibitive, is uncertain. Whatever the cause women were not encouraged to enroll in geology and were actively discouraged from majoring in it. Geology is a dangerous profession because of the many natural hazards that can occur in the field, such as rock falls, volcanic eruptions, landslides, wild animal attacks and drownings. As such it was not thought suitable for women, and only about

4% of bachelor's degrees in geology were awarded to women from the time degree records were kept by sex, beginning in 1948, through 1960. But this changed slowly, beginning in the 1960s, so that women earned 9% of bachelor's degrees during that decade, and that proportion increased throughout the 1970s and early 1980s to 24% in 1986. Higher degree levels show similar increases, with 1986 degree figures showing that women earned 23.6% of master's degrees and 21.6% of Ph.D.s (American Geological Institute 1987).

The beginnings of the women's movement in the 1960s, coupled with a gradual understanding by girls and young women that they needed to prepare themselves for the world of work, brought increasing numbers of women into college, and thus into science and engineering fields. As women increasingly demanded fair and equitable treatment the larger society began to question many discriminatory practices which had been taken for granted, such as higher entrance requirements for women than for men and quotas that excluded qualified women (Hornig 1984). Laws were passed and executive orders signed to require non-discrimination in educational opportunities in schools at all levels where federal funding occurred. New laws also forbade unequal treatment in employment by employers who received federal funds.

Differential treatment of men and women did not immediately disappear. Indeed some of the equalization benefits of Title IX of the Amendments to the Education Act that had been believed were inherent in the legislation were later withdrawn by the courts. Nonetheless, the issues of fairness and equity that were involved became the subject of debate and compromise. Among women in the science fields these issues were recognized by the early 1970s, as evidenced by the number of committees, caucuses, and women's organizations which originated during this period (Briscoe 1978). The continuing vitality of these organizations in 1987 is evidence that equality of opportunity has not yet been achieved but throughout the decade of the seventies, and into the early eighties, women continued to prepare themselves at an unprecedented rate to enter the professional work force, including the scientific professions. But the number attracted to careers in the physical sciences continued to be small relative to the numbers who began preparation for entry into the life science and social science professions.

From 1950 to 1985 women earned 9,600 doctorates in the physical and mathematical sciences. Their share of these science doctorates increased from 3.7% of the total in the 1950s to 13.8% in the 1980–85 period. But even in 1985 women earned only one in six of these degrees, a figure far lower than in any other science field.

Most of the increase in all science and engineering degrees, and particularly the increase in degrees in mathematical and physical sciences, can be attributed to an increase in the proportion of women completing degrees in any fields. Between 1973 and 1986 women increased their share of all earned degrees from 43.8% to 50.8% at the bachelor's level; from 41.4% to 50.3% at the master's level (NCES 1973–87); and from 18% to 35.2% of doctorates (NRC 1974–87). In physical and mathematical sciences their proportion rose from 16.6% to 35.7% of bachelor's degrees; from 14.6% to 28.9% of master's degrees; and from 9.6% to 16.3% of Ph.D.s during that decade (NSF 1982, NCES 1982–87 and NRC 1983–87).

Because of the rapid increase both in the actual number of degree awards in science and engineering earned by women, and their increasing proportion of all degrees in these fields, the assumption is common that women have moved out of their more traditional fields and into the non-traditional ones. This is not the case. As shown in Figure 1, the proportion of women Ph.D.s who earned their degrees in engineering, mathematics and the physical sciences (the EMP fields) actually *dropped* throughout the seventies, only rising in 1985 to match the proportion choosing these fields in 1970 (Figure 1). The increase in engineering doctorates earned by women was accompanied by a similar decrease in the physical sciences and the math/computer sciences (NRC 1971–87).

Among all women who earned bachelor's degrees the proportion earned in any science or engineering field increased from 19.9% in 1970 to 25% in 1985. But the increase in the physical/mathematical/computer sciences group is small — from 3.9% in 1970 to 5% in 1985.

Within this group the increase in both degrees and proportionate share of degrees for women in computer science is matched by an equivalent drop in mathematics degrees. As a percentage of all mathematics, statistics and computer science bachelor's degrees awarded to women, the computer science component was 1.9% in 1970, and 69% in 1985. The actual number of degree awards in these combined fields dropped through 1978 despite a

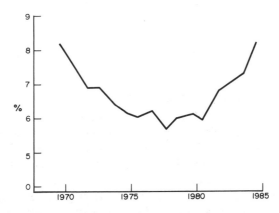

Fig. 1. Proportion of Ph.D.s Earned by Women in the EMP Fields, 1970–85

large increase in the number of women earning bachelor's degrees during that period. But from 1978 to 1985 the numerical increase was rapid for both men and women.

Perhaps because of the employment reductions in the computer industry in 1984 and 1985, the proportion of male freshmen who plan to major in computer science dropped from 5.4% in 1983 to 2.6% in fall 1986. For freshmen women the drop in those two years is from 3.7% to 1.6%. There is no commensurate increase in the number of freshmen planning to major in mathematics. Both in 1983 and in 1986, 0.8% of men and 0.8% of women indicated a probable major in this field (Astin et al. 1983–87).

As a proportion of total graduates who choose to major in a particular field freshman plans are a fairly good indicator of bachelor's degrees four years later, (Vetter 1986 unpublished). Based on those plans, we can expect that no more than 1% of the women bachelor's graduates in 1989 will have majored in the physical sciences — about the same proportion that has chosen these fields for the past two decades. About 2.4% will have majored in mathematics, statistics or computer sciences, compared with 4.4% of the class of 1986. Because the 1989 graduating class is expected to be about 6% smaller than the 1986 class (NCES 1982) — a difference of about 29,000 women graduates — the number of women graduates in math/computer science fields could drop from a high of about 22,400 in 1986 to only 9,600 in 1989. The number of women earning bachelor's degrees in the physical sciences should be about 4,800.

Both because of the shrinking college age group and because of the lesser interest in physical and mathematical sciences, it appears evident that both the numerical and the proportional increases in women preparing to enter these science fields has ended. Women now earn slightly more than half of the bachelor's and master's degrees awarded by U.S. universities, so that no further increase will result from equalizing their proportionate share of all graduates. The size of the age 22 population cohort is already shrinking, and will continue to do so through the 1990s.

The increasing numbers of women earning degrees, including science and engineering degrees, from 1970 through 1986 would seem to indicate that educational opportunities for women have equalized with opportunities for men, and that the fact that women are earning only a small fraction of the physical science degrees is a matter of their personal choice, no matter how much that choice is affected by societal assumptions about appropriate careers for women. But despite immense progress equalization of opportunity in academe does not yet exist, even for students. The remaining differences are more subtle today than in earlier years.

For example, among persons who earned a Ph.D. in the physical sciences in 1985, a higher proportion of the men (74%) than of the women (69%) had research assistantships. Women were somewhat more likely than men to have teaching assistantships to support their graduate work.

The increasing proportion of foreign-born male faculty in the physical and mathematical science fields is a continuing problem for women students, since, in addition to the obvious language problems, most such faculty come from cultures where women are perceived and treated differently than in the United States (Hall 1985).

Despite these continuing problems, and others including sexual harassment (Sandler 1986), the educational climate for women is much improved over the past 15 years. Continued improvement will probably result from the efforts by universities to attract good students from a shrinking population of college-age Americans.

But even with the additional opportunities that may result from the smaller college age group there is serious doubt that women will continue to expand into physical and mathematical science fields, even at a reduced rate of increase. Recent evidence indicates that as women have reached their half of bachelor's and master's degrees, their rate of increase in science and engineering has leveled off and in some fields appears to be turning down. In engineering for example, where women increased from 2% of entering freshmen in fall 1970 to 17% in fall 1983, their proportion of the fall 1984 class dropped to 16.5%, remaining at that level in fall 1985 (EMC 1972–86). This small decrease might be thought to be insignificant except that it is verified by the announced plans of freshman women, who indicated less interest in engineering in the past two years than in previous years. The proportionate decline in the percentage of freshman women planning majors in computer science and physical science indicates that the numbers of women completing degrees in those fields may also shrink faster than the total graduating classes over the next decade.

There are several reasons why these changes may be taking place. Opportunities in the marketplace, though somewhat improved for women, continue to lag behind those for men. A number of active programs to recruit women into science and engineering have been dropped, such as the NSF program in the late 1970s that sponsored workshops for women in science. In general the professional community of scientists in these fields has made little effort to welcome women into their fraternity, particularly in those fields where few women worked before 1970. Whatever the reasons, the marked increases in participation of women in science and engineering, and to a lesser degree in the physical sciences, that have occurred over the past 15 years appear to be at or near an end

Because of the length of the educational pipeline the proportion of women earning Ph.D.s in science and engineering should continue to increase for a few more years. From fall 1977 to fall 1986 the proportion of women among full-time students in doctoral-granting institutions who were majoring in EMP fields increased from 12.0% to 17.5%. As these graduate students complete their highest degrees the proportion of women in succeeding student groups probably will remain stable.

EMPLOYMENT

Prepared with the necessary education credentials women have been moving into the science labor force in record numbers over the past decade. Women are about 12% of physical scientists, 21% of mathematical scientists, and 26% of computer scientists (NSF 1986). In the doctorate population, women are 7.8% of physical scientists, 9.7% of mathematicians and 10.9% of computer scientists (NSF 1987). Although their opportunities for participation have increased substantially over the past decade by almost any statistical parameters they have not yet reached equality with men having similar credentials. The differences are substantial between men and women in unemployment rates, opportunities to find jobs in science or engineering, opportunities for full-time work, opportunities for academic tenure, and salary levels. Some of these differences are attributable to the more recent entry of women into the labor force. But even when factors such as years of experience, employment sector and degree level are controlled, differences remain, and all of them are negative for women.

UNEMPLOYMENT

Women science graduates experience more difficulty in finding appropriate employment after graduation than do the men with whom they graduate. In 1985 higher proportions of new women doctorates than men were still seeking employment at the time the degree was awarded — 13% of women and 10.4% of men in the physical sciences; 20.8% and 17.2% in mathematics; and 24.2% and 18% respectively in computer sciences (NRC 1987).

At lower degree levels women also continue to experience more difficulty than their male classmates in finding employment in their fields after they graduate (NSF 1986). Their unemployment rates are higher, they are less likely to find jobs in science or engineering, and they have fewer opportunities for full time work than the men from their classes.

Women have higher unemployment rates than men in each of these fields, at each degree level, and at every experience level. Among chemistry doctorates in 1985 women were 8.4% of the labor force, but 16.2% were involuntarily unemployed (NRC 1986 unpublished). In mathematics women were 9% of the labor force and 19.8% of those seeking employment. Even in computer science women were 9.4% of the doctoral labor force and 28.6% of the small group who were unemployed and seeking work.

In each of seven biennial surveys of the doctoral population since 1973 the National Research Council has found unemployment rates for women to be two to five times higher than for men, with some variation by field. Generally the higher the unemployment rate for men the wider the gap in unemployment rates between men and women, seeming to indicate that women have more difficulty finding jobs in a tight job market than men (NRC 1984 and 1986, unpublished).

Among those who find employment women continue to fare less well than men in terms of status or rank, tenure or other job security, salary and promotion, whatever their employment sector.

Regardless of field, women scientists, particularly at the doctoral level, are more likely than men to work in academic institutions, hospitals and clinics, non-profit organizations and state and local governments. They are less likely than men to be employed in industry or in the federal government. Nonetheless, men are still more likely than women to be hired for academic tenure track positions, to be promoted to tenure and to achieve full professorships. Women hold assistant professorships and nonfaculty positions more than twice as often as men, and there has been little change in these distributions since 1977 (NRC 1978, 1980, 1982, 1984 and 1986, unpublished).

The Women Chemists' Committee of the American Chemical Society found that in 1983 women held only 188 of 4,400 faculty positions in chemistry departments that grant doctorates (4.1%) although women have earned 9.5% of all doctorates in chemistry awarded by these universities in the past 20 years, and 14% of those awarded over the past decade (Vetter and Babco 1986). In industry doctorate women chemists remain under-represented by about 50% (NRC 1980).

In 1980, 8% of men and 30% of women chemists employed in Ph.D.-granting universities were in non-professorial positions. By 1985 those figures had risen to 14% of men and 49% of women. The fraction holding the rank of instructor doubled for both sexes from 1980 to 1984: from 2% to 4% for men; from 6% to 12% for women (ACS 1986).

Even marital status reflects the differential opportunities for women. Among members of the American Chemical Society in 1985, 17% of the men and 40% of the women were not currently married (ACS 1986). Among all women doctorates in the physical and mathematical sciences 32% were single in 1985.

One in five of the academically employed scientists and engineers at colleges and universities in 1985 was a woman (NSF 1985b, unpublished), but women's share of faculty positions, tenured positions and tenure track positions was far less.

Among all academically employed doctoral scientists and engineers in 1985, 63% of men but only 38% of women were tenured. An additional 16% of men and 23% of women were on the tenure track, while 14% of men and 31% of women were neither tenured nor in tenure track positions. Although proportions differ by field the gap exists across all fields. For example, 33% of women in physics and astronomy are neither tenured nor on a tenure track, compared with 19% of men. In chemistry the proportions are 39.5% and 14.6% respectively; in computer sciences, 18% and 14%; in earth and environmental sciences, 37% and 18%. Only in mathematics are the proportions similar — 15.7% and 15.1% (NRC 1986, unpublished).

The differential is not just a function of age. Among those aged 36–45 in 1983, one in four women (26%) compared with one in ten men (11%) was neither tenured nor on a tenure track (NRC 1984). Inequities in the early career stages continue to affect women scientists as they move forward.

Even with tenure women move up the professorial ranks more slowly than men. Among academically employed doctoral scientists and engineers in 1983 who earned their doctorates during the decade of the sixties, 70.5% of the men but only 41.8% of the women had reached the rank of professor. For those who earned the doctorate between 1970 and 1975, 25% of the men but only 14.7% of the women had achieved the top rank.

In industry men are considerably more likely than women at similar experience levels to be engaged in management, whether in research and development, or other management (NSF 1986). Women, particularly at the doctoral level, are under-represented in industry (NRC 1980).

Women scientists are fairly well represented in government employment in almost all fields. But women's average civil service grades (and thus salary) are well below those of men in the same field. For example, women are 21.1% of federal chemists, but their average salaries are only 80.4% of average salaries earned by men chemists (Babco 1987).

SALARIES

Women's salaries reflect their lesser opportunities for advancement. They earn less than men in every field of science, in every employment sector, at every degree level, and at every level of experience, although there is some recent evidence that this may be changing for women who have entered the labor force in the past decade.

Beginning salaries of men and women graduates at the end of the bachelor's degree are more nearly in balance than at any later career stage. In 1986 average salary offers to women bachelor's graduates were 98.6% of offers to men in chemistry, 97.9% in computer sciences, 98.4% in mathematics, and 98.3% in other physical and earth sciences. The dollar differences range from $324 to $552 per year (College Placement Council 1986).

Regardless of degree level, field or type of employer, salary differences between men and women increase with additional years of experience. For example, in 1985 women bachelor's-level chemists employed full-time in industry who had earned their bachelor's degrees 2–4 years earlier earned 97.5% of men's salaries. Those whose bachelor's degrees were awarded

20–24 years earlier earned only 82.9% as much as men (American Chemical Society 1985).

Despite a decade of affirmative action there appears to be little improvement in the ratio of doctorate women's to men's salaries during that time. Among doctoral chemists in 1985 women with one or less years of experience averaged 94.9% of salaries paid to men at the same experience level. As at other degree levels the salary gap which exists in every field at the start of a Ph.D. career in science widens with age. At the 10–14-year experience level women chemists' salaries were 86.7% of men's; and at the 15–19-year level, 81.7% — a dollar difference of $8,900 per year. Women doctoral physicists at the 2–4-year experience level earned 92.9% men's salaries; and at the 10–14-year experience level, 86.7%. For mathematical scientists the ratios at those two levels are 95.9% and 94.9%. Similar comparisons for environmental scientists are 95.1% and 94.1% (National Research Council 1986, unpublished).

SUMMARY AND CONCLUSIONS

Despite evidence of continuing inequality for those women who have entered the physical and mathematical science community, as shown by unemployment rates, academic rank and salary levels, women have made some progress in increasing their participation in these fields over the past decade at every degree level, and in every employment sector.

Also on the positive side is evidence that an increasing proportion of pre-college women are taking the essential high school courses in mathematics and science that will hold open the option of choosing to pursue a science career (The College Board 1980–86). On the other hand there is also evidence that the steady increase in the proportion of women earning baccalaureate degrees in science and engineering has already leveled off in a number of fields, and freshman interest in a major in physical science, math or computer science has dropped sharply in the past two years.

Some increase in graduate level participation through the rest of the decade is indicated by both bachelor's degrees and graduate enrollment patterns. Women continue to show steady increases in their proportion of graduate students in these fields, rising from 18.4% of all graduate students in all institutions in fall 1977 to 24.6% in fall 1984 (NSF 1986a). But reduced participation of undergraduate women will affect graduate participation in just a few years.

At the employment level some progress is indicated by the fact that among all scientists in these fields who are employed in academic institutions in 1985, 14.3% are women, up from 9.3% in 1974. Of course a significantly higher proportion of these women than of the men are in temporary positions outside a tenure track.

Not so positive is the fact that less than 8% of all academically employed doctorates in physical sciences, mathematical and computer sciences and environmental sciences are women, even in 1985. At the same time women earned 16.4% of all Ph.D.s awarded in these fields in 1985, and have earned 12.3% of all those awarded for a decade (NRC 1987). Women are only 7% of doctoral scientists in these fields who are employed in industry in 1985. They are only 6.6% of those employed in federal, state or local government. They are 9.9% of those employed by non-profit organizations (NSF 1987).

But women were 37.6% of all doctoral scientists in these fields who were employed outside of science or engineering, and 63.2% of the number who gave as the reason for such employment that no science or engineering job was available (NRC 1986, unpublished). Even though the numbers are small (593 employed outside of science and engineering, and 38 who list lack of a science or engineering job as the cause), the high proportion of these groups that are women, compared to their availability in these fields and their proportion in science jobs, indicates lack of equality in employment opportunities for women.

Women are still a rarity among scientists recognized for excellence, but a small number have risen to the top.

- There are now 51 women members of the National Academy of Sciences, or 3.5% of the total membership of 1,477. Only 60 women have been elected since the Academy's founding in 1863, but three of the 59 new members elected in 1986 are women.

- Several of the major scientific societies, including the American Association for the Advancement of Science, The American Physical Society, the American Astronomical Society, and the American Chemical Society, now have or have recently had women presidents.

- Two women have been recognized with a Nobel prize in science in the past decade, although no women have won the prize in chemistry or physics since 1964. Nobel laureates generally are honored for work done many years earlier.

- In recent years 35–47% of Westinghouse Talent Search finalists have been female, although no woman has yet represented the United States in the International Mathematics Olympiad (Malcom 1983).

Some continuing increases in the participation of women in the physical sciences are probable but almost certainly such increases will come even more slowly than has occurred in the past 15 years. Future increases are not assured and even some gains of the past decade may not last. These gains have occurred in a positive policy climate of legalized opportunities for educational access, supportive changes in society's view of the role of women, and favorable political backing. A change in this climate, to hostile or even to neutral, might be expected to slow further women's proportionate growth in the physical sciences as well as their continued reach toward equality.

In the physical sciences women are not yet a critical mass large enough to influence the discipline in a significant way. None of the current indicators of future participation promises much hope that this objective might be achieved in this century.

REFERENCES

American Chemical Society. 1986. *Women Chemists 1985*, A Supplemental Report on the American Chemical Society's 1985 Survey of Salaries and Employment. Washington D.C.: American Chemical Society.

American Chemical Society. 1985. *Salaries, 1985*. Washington D.C.: American Chemical Society.

American Geological Institute. 1987. Enrollments and Degrees in the Geosciences, 1985–86, unpublished.

American Institute of Physics. 1986. *Society Membership Profile: The Pattern of Subfield Associations*. New York: American Institute of Physics.

Astin, Alexander et al. 1974–86. *The American Freshman: National Norms for Fall 1973 – Fall 1986*. Los Angeles: American Council on Education/Cooperative Educational Research Program, University of California, Los Angeles Graduate School of Education.

Babco, Eleanor. 1985. *Salaries of Scientists, Engineers and Technicians*, Thirteenth Edition. Washington D.C.: Commission on Professionals in Science and Technology.

Briscoe, Anne. 1978. Phenomenon of the Seventies: The Women's Caucuses. *Signs, Journal of Women in Culture and Society*, **4,** No. 1, 152–158. Chicago: University of Chicago.

The College Board. 1980–86. *National College-Bound Seniors 1979* through *1985*. New York: Admissions Testing Program of the College Board.

College Placement Council. 1974–86. *A Study of Beginning Offers, Final Report, July 1975* through *July 1986*. Bethlehem, Pennsylvania: College Placement Council.

Engineering Manpower Commission. 1972–86. *Engineering Enrollments, Fall 1981* through *Fall 1985*. New York and Washington D.C.: American Association of Engineering Societies.

Engineering Manpower Commission. 1983–86. *Engineering and Technology Degrees 1982* through *1985*. New York and Washington D.C.: American Association of Engineering Societies.

Hall, Roberta. 1985. Foreign Faculty and Graduate Students: How Do They Affect the Learning Climate for Women? *The International Flow of Scientific Talent: Data, Policies and Issues*. Washington D.C.: Scientific Manpower Commission.

Hornig, Lilli S. 1984. Women in science and engineering: Why so few? *Technology Review* **87,** No. 8, 29–41.

Malcom, S. M. 1983. An *Assessment of Programs that Facilitate Increased Access and Achievement of Female and Minorities in K-12 Mathematics and Science Education*, Washington D.C. American Association for the Advancement of Science, Office of Applications in Science, 31 July.

National Center for Education Statistics. 1972–86. *Earned Degrees Conferred by Institutions of Higher Education, United States, 1969–70* through *1979–80*, Washington D.C.: Government Printing Office, 1972 through 1982. *1980–81* through *1985–86*, unpublished.

National Center for Education Statistics. 1982a. *Projections of Education Statistics to 1990–91* (NCES 81–402A), Department of Education, Washington D.C.: U.S. Government Printing Office.

National Research Council. 1973. Doctorates Awarded from 1920 to 1971 by Subfield of Doctorate, Sex and Decade. Doctorate Records file, unpublished.

National Research Council. 1971–87. *Summary Report, 1970* through *1985 Doctorate Recipients from United States Universities*, Washington D.C.: National Academy of Sciences.

National Research Council. 1974, 1976, 1978, 1980, 1982, 1984, 1986 unpublished. *Science and Engineering Doctorates in the United States, 1973 Profile* and *1975 Profile; Science, Engineering and Humanities Doctorates in the United States, 1977 Profile, 1979 Profile, 1981*

32   B. M. VETTER

Profile and *1983 Profile*. Data from 1985 Profile unpublished. Washington D.C.: National Academy of Sciences.

National Research Council. 1980. *Women Scientists in Industry and Government — How Much Progress in the 1970's?* Washington D.C., National Academy of Sciences.

National Science Foundation. 1982. *Science and Engineering Degrees: 1950–80* (NSF 82-307), Washington D.C.: U.S. Government Printing Office.

National Science Foundation. 1982, 1984 and 1986. *U.S. Scientists and Engineers, 1980* (NSF 82-314), *1982* (NSF 84-321) and *1984*. Washington D.C.: U.S. Government Printing Office.

National Science Foundation. 1985. *Science and Engineering Personnel: A National Overview*, (NSF 85-302), Washington, D.C.: U.S. Government Printing Office.

National Science Foundation. 1986a. *Academic Science/Engineering Graduate Enrollment and Support Fall 1984, Detailed Statistical Tables*. Washington, D.C.: U.S. Government Printing Office.

National Science Foundation. 1986b. *Women and Minorities in Science and Engineering*, Washington D.C.: U.S. Government Printing Office, January.

National Science Foundation. 1987. *Characteristics of Doctoral Scientists and Engineers in the United States, 1985*. Washington D.C.: National Science Foundation.

Rossiter, Margaret W. 1982. *Women Scientists in America: Struggles and Strategies to 1940*. Baltimore: Johns Hopkins University Press.

Rubin, Vera. 1986. Women's Work, *Science 86*, **7**, No. 6, July/August 1986, 58–65.

Sandler, Bernice. 1986. *The Campus Climate Revisited: Chilly for Women Faculty, Administrators, and Graduate Students*. Washington D.C.: Project on the Status and Education of Women, Association of American Colleges.

Vetter, Betty, and Babco, Eleanor L. 1987. *Professional Women and Minorities: A Manpower Data Resource Service*, Seventh Edition. Washington D.C.: Commission on Professionals in Science and Technology.

Vetter, Betty. 1980. Working women scientists and engineers. *Science*, **207**, 4 January, 28–34.

Vetter, Betty. 1984. Women and minorities in chemistry. *Professional Relations Bulletin of the American Chemical Society*, **33**, June, 8–9.

Vetter, Betty. 1986. Freshman Plans Compared with Bachelor's Degrees Four Years Later, unpublished.

Chapter 2

Gender Bias in Archeology: Here, Then and Now*

Joan M. Gero

INTRODUCTION: FEMALE ROLES IN THE PREHISTORIC RECORD

Archeologists, as explorers and discoverers, have maintained the myth of objective research far longer than researchers in other social science disciplines. As scholars of "mankind" archeologists have dabbled little in self-reflective criticism, seldom wishing to examine how the knowledge that they produce and the professional world they create and operate in are both underwritten by a present ideology.

In this chapter I argue that archeologists have systematically misinterpreted and ignored the archeological evidence for production by women in prehistory, and that female archeologists today are similarly being denied access to productive processes in the archeological enterprise. First I will look at how unexamined assumptions about gender affect our interpretations of the past, turning then to how these same assumptions affect the gender relations among archeologists today, producing and reproducing, in our prehistoric interpretations and in our professional lives, the same society, past and present.

The delayed concern with an archeological study of gender (Conkey 1982; Conkey and Spector 1984) has been stimulated by the publication, in the past decade, of literally hundreds of books and articles written from a

*This chapter emerges directly from two earlier pieces of work (see Gero 1983 and 1985). Since then I have suggested to the Anthropology program at NSF some additional research that would be most informative in updating and interpreting the percentages of successful vs. unsuccessful male and female grant awards, information which is not public and which cannot be undertaken without NSF's cooperation. But since no further statistical research on this division of labor has been conducted at NSF, I have decided to let the earlier dates stand as originally researched, since at least they relate to the same span of years and are therefore integrated and coherent, rather than presenting different dates for different parts of the argument.

feminist perspective. Archeologists might have responded earlier and, like the socio-cultural anthropologists, participated more actively in the climate of interest in gender had it not been for the profession's traditional concerns and practices which offered very low or even negative prestige for engaging in this discourse. Historically conservative, the archeological enterprise is also dominated by white middle-class males (Kelley and Hanen, in press) and among them a stereotypic self-image as "masculine," "strong," and "active" prevails (Woodall and Perricone 1981). This community was slow to embrace a feminist perspective.

Conkey and Spector (1984), however, have recently offered a significant analysis of how gender ideology is manifested in archeological research. As Conkey and Spector (1984:5) point out, gender assertions have been made regularly in reconstructions of the past, although such assertions "are so implicit as to be excluded from the attempts of archeologists to confirm and validate them." Drawn in part from androcentric ethnographies and in part from the personal experiences of most archeologists as modern males in a state level society, the implicit gender models reconstruct male and female roles in the past much as they are stereotyped today: females, if noted, perform a narrow range of passive, home oriented tasks in contrast to their public, productive and far-ranging male counterparts.

Conkey and Spector (1984:5–14) go on to provide examples of how archeological interpretations of gender roles in the past have been skewed by the presentist ideology. Not only have grave goods been interpreted differently when recovered from male versus female burial contexts (pestles found with female burials are evidence of grinding and food processing, while pestles in male burials suggest the *production* of pestles or use as hammerstones in other productive activities, in Winters 1968:206), but the very basis of human existence now rests on reconstructions of a strict sexual division of labor that is extended back to a proto-human era. In this scenario food-sharing and a shared home base combine to place the increasingly encumbered, restricted, passive, and sedentary female at the roots of humankind (Conkey and Spector 1984:8–9). Even the language applied to archeological interpretations of male behaviors differs from that applied to female behaviors: males perform "activities" while females engage in "tasks," and descriptions of male activities " are more detailed, and are portrayed more actively and more frequently than female-associated activities. There is asymmetry in the visibility, energy levels, accomplishments, and contributions of the sexes" (Conkey and Spector 1984:10).

It is clear that a set of unexamined assumptions about gender has crept into archeological interpretation while explicit attention to women's roles in the archeological past has been all but lacking. The androcentric interpretation and presentation of the past is both structured by, but also fed into, the larger ideological and symbolic domain of our contemporary society, as the past duplicates and legitimates the present-day norms and values.

ARCHEOLOGICAL RESEARCH AND GENDER

The gender ideology we impose on the past derives from a present context in which we live and work, and we can expect archeologists to conform in their professional roles to the same ideology that is adopted to explain the past. Following this reasoning we are alerted to certain strong parallels between the males reconstructed to inhabit and dominate the archeological record . . . and the practicing field archeologists themselves!

You are probably familiar with the archeologist portrayed in the character of Indiana Jones: a swaggering, danger-defying macho-man, sweating in the heat of the underdeveloped landscape, with pith helmet and spade, bull whip ready, caught up in the lure of the unknown past in a perpetual treasure hunt for lost cities and beautiful relics. "ARCHEOLOGISTS ARE THE COWBOYS OF SCIENCE!" declares a bumber sticker in Alaska, and the cigarette and booze ads, the wrist watch ads, and the ads for field clothes, all present the rugged features of an obvious field archeologist wresting our past from the ground: outdoorsy, strong, fit, and 100% MALE. Note how closely this image matches the archetypical reconstruction of Man-the-Hunter as physically active, rugged, exploratory, dominant and risk-taking, the one who brings home the goodies. The archeologist, in fact, inextricably intertwined with Man-the-Hunter, embodies our cultural and economic ideals of the masculine role. He takes his data RAW!

Where, then, are the females of this archeologist species? Corresponding to the stereotyped male role, we expect to find the female archeologist secluded in the base-camp laboratory or museum, sorting and preparing archeological materials for consumption. If traditional economic and cultural stereotypes prevail, she will be indoors, private and protected, passively receptive, ordering and systematizing, her feminine skills supported but without recognized contribution to the productive process. The woman-at-home archeologist must fulfil her stereotypic feminine role by specializing in the analysis of archeological materials, typologizing, seriating, studying wear or paste or iconographic motifs. She will have to do the archeological housework; she will have to cook the data!

If this sexual division of labor actually exists in archeological research, then male archeologists will be concentrated in field-based research, undertaking projects which include the collection of primary data from excavations or surveys. Female archeologists, on the other hand, will be involved in non-field projects, projects where the investigator analyzes data that she/he did not collect from an archeological context, and where data collection is not a significant aspect of the research.

A rapid survey of relevant statistics convincingly documents this sexual division of labor. Most informally, I have reviewed current Mesoamerican research for four years, as self-reported in the 1967, 1968, 1979 and 1980 issues of *American Antiquity*, the most prestigious professional journal in new world archeology today. Despite short-comings of representativeness this sample encompasses a wide diversity of active archeological personnel, one that is preselected by no other criteria than a common research focus on Mexico and Central America. Statistics from this sample show that of the 149 fieldwork projects listed in these four years, 120 are directed by males while only 29 projects have female directors, of whom nine are actually co-directors with males (usually their husbands). If the co-directed projects are removed from our counts (see Table 2.1), a ratio of more than 5:1 male-to-female field directors results. We can also note from Table 2.1 that all of the North American male archeologists working in Mesoamerica, 85% of the 1967/68 group, and 76% of the 1979/80 group were involved in fieldwork, while only 15% of the earlier sample of North American women working in Mesoamerica, and 24% of the later group were collecting their own primary data from the field.

The same division of labor is reflected in recently completed archeology dissertations compiled from *Dissertation Abstracts International*. At the expense of not reflecting discipline-wide activity these statistics offer a very contemporary view of current developments in archeology. Without addressing the separate but obviously relevant question of why 160 males and only 60 females completed dissertations in the same selection of sample years, we find that 63% of the dissertations by males are based on original fieldwork, while only 32% of the dissertations by females are based on original fieldwork projects. Differences between male and female populations of dissertation writers is significant at the .0001 level!

Finally a third measure, based on the distribution of National Science Foundation funds for archeology, was taken from the published 1967, 1968, 1979 and 1980 published National Science Foundation *Grants and Awards* reports. Since the funding behind these projects is among the most prestigious funding available for archeological research we can expect the discipline's norms and values to be exaggerated in this measure. From the data presented in the last two columns of Table 2, we calculate that 73% of all the funded grants during these years went toward fieldwork projects, while only 27% supported *all* other classes of archeological research combined: collections analysis, archeometry, ethnoarcheology, ethno-history, curation and archival publication. Thus NSF consistently over-represents fieldwork in the grants it awards in comparison, say, with the population of dissertation writers: 87% of the males funded by NSF did fieldwork (compared with 63% of the male dissertation writers), and 57% of the females funded by NSF did fieldwork (as compared to 32% of the female dissertation writers). While males still dominate fieldwork in very

TABLE 2.1. *Males and Females Conducting Field-Based and Non-Field-Based Archeological Research, Assessed by Three Different Measures*

| | CURRENT MESOAMERICAN RESEARCH REPORTED IN AMERICAN ANTIQUITY | | | | DISSERTATION ABSTRACTS INTERNATIONAL† | | | | NATIONAL SCIENCE FOUNDATION GRANTS AND AWARDS† | | | |
| | MALES | | FEMALES | | MALES | | FEMALES | | MALES | | FEMALES | |
	Field	Non-Field	Field	Non-Field	Field	Non-Field	Field	Non-Field	Field	Non-Field	Field	Non-Field
1967-	85%	15%	75%	25%	84%	16%	75%	25%	88%	12%	88%	12%
1968	n=29	n=5	n=3	n=1	n=31	n=6	n=3	n=1	n=75	n=10	n=7	n=1
1979-	76%	24%	44%	56%	63%	37%	32%	68%	87%	13%	57%	43%
1980	n=82	n=27	n=17	n=22	n=78	n=45	n=18	n=38	n=55	n=8	n=4	n=3

* In all the tabulated statistics, projects undertaken by male-and-female teams have been omitted. Projects undertaken by more than one male (or female) are conservatively counted as a single male (or female) project.

† In *Dissertation Abstracts International* and NSF *Grants and Awards*, the gender of some investigators and the nature of some research projects could not be ascertained. This small number of cases, never exceeding 3.8% of the data/year, is omitted from these counts.

significant proportions, once sufficiently large sample sizes are attained in both groups, the emphasis on fieldwork as the definitional and most prestigious archeological enterprise leaves the larger population of women especially alienated from the main core of research personnel and interests.

Let us sum up the more recent data: in the years 1979–80 males, who represent 74% of the total sample of archeologists counted here, account for 83% of all the current Mesoamerican field research, 81% of the dissertations based on field research, and 93% of all the NSF field research projects. Females on the other hand, representing 26% of the total sample here, undertake 45% of the current Mesoamerican non-field research, 46% of the non-field-based dissertations, and a more proportional 27% of the undervalued NON-field research funded by NSF.

A longer, more developmental look at the gender division in archeology was also attempted. For this dissertation abstracts were again selected since they offered the most accessible, most inclusive, and most sensitive data base for research done in archeology. All abstracts from the last 25 years of dissertations in anthropological archeology were examined (Table 2.2). Note again that the tiny sample of females receiving doctorates in archeology before 1970 makes comparisons unreliable for these years, and the apparent inconsistencies in the two earliest five-year periods, 1960–64 and 1965–69, are obviously a function of sample size. My own hunch is that in 1960–64, where the research of only three female archeologists can be tallied, we are actually seeing an *un*representative picture of females doing

TABLE 2.2. *Males' and Females' Dissertation Research from 25 years of Dissertation Abstracts Internationals*

	MALES		FEMALES	
	Field	Non-Field	Field	Non-Field
1960–64	62% n=18	38% n=11	33% n=1	67% n=2
1965–69	73% n=61	27% n=22	75% n=6	25% n=2
1970-74	68% n=141	32% n=66	29% n=13	71% n=32
1975–79	61% n=176	39% n=112	37% n=49	63% n=83
1980–84*	62% n=176	38% n=107	34% n=60	66% n=115

* For 1984, only the months of January through July are included in these counts.

more non-field research, because I suspect that in those years, males and females were fulfilling very similar research roles, typically involving a heavy emphasis on fieldwork, as is evident in the slightly larger sample from the 1965–69 period.

As soon as women enter the profession in larger numbers, however, after 1970, the trend is unambiguous. Very close to two-thirds of the female archeologists base their dissertation research on non-field-oriented, analytic projects, while very close to two-thirds of the males undertake field-related research. We can also extrapolate from this sequence that in the last 10 years, males have dropped from conducting between 92% and 95% (in 1960–74) to only 75%–78% of the field-based dissertation research (in 1975–84). But this shift is fully accounted for by the swelling of the female doctorate ranks, where consistent proportions of field and non-field research are maintained but larger numbers of females contribute to field research each year.

Taking all these statistics together, it seems evident that archeological field research, fulfilling a male stereotype, is indeed associated with male archeologists. Moreover male-dominated field research is precisely the aspect of archeology most heavily emphasized and rewarded by the prestigious, state-controlled National Science Foundation, an observation offered independently by M. Conkey (1978:5). This brings us to the very important question of whether women *want* to work in the field, and here I rely on data generously supplied by John Yellen, director of the Anthropology Program at the National Science Foundation (see also Yellen 1983). Yellen reports that in 1979–80, males accounted for 85% of the fieldwork grant applications, but that the success rates of these fieldwork applications was 35% for male applicants while females were only 15% or less than half as successful. On the other hand females were 28% successful if they followed their stereotyped sex roles and sought non-field-related research funds. Unlike females, the success rate for males were unaffected by the nature of the proposed project. The archeological community and the old-boy, male-dominated networking system seem to support women-at-home, but discourage female entry into the field.

A few more facts: in archeology, overall NSF applications by men are significantly more successful than applications by women. Even in the area where women tend to specialize, collections analysis, the average funding over the sampled years shows a female's grant to be $2,100 LESS than the average male's collections analysis grant. Worse still, the discrepancy in average NSF field project grants for males and females is a full $11,550.00. Finally, these statistics are uniquely true for archeology and do not hold in either social or biological anthropology (Yellen 1983:60).

We conclude that if women are applying to do fieldwork in smaller numbers than males they are also being excluded from the field, and if they receive fieldwork funding they get less of it.

J. M. GERO
CROSS-CULTURAL EXAMINATION OF WOMEN IN ARCHEOLOGY

The above statistics show that idealized sex-role definitions are realities in the institution of North American archeology. But why are these idealized sex roles used and maintained in our professional society? Who do they serve and how have they developed? Here I want to follow two different routes of inquiry. First it will be informative (to say nothing of knee-jerk anthropological) to do a cross-cultural comparison, to see if these patterns of sexual divisions hold in archeological communities outside North America. In asking whether gender bias is universal in archeology, we are in effect asking whether masculinity and femininity have the same meaning and the same weight in all cultural contexts. Moreover, we will want to address the implicit claim that many of the tasks involved in directing large-scale archeological field research are areas that females are unequipped to handle. Following this we will want to ask, in light of our findings, how our own pattern of sexual segregation is maintained and reproduced within this scientific community. Towards these goals I collected data on archeological sex roles in South America, homeland of *machismo*.

Neither grants nor dissertations could be used as a data base for assessing archeological gender roles in South America since both grants and dissertations are rare commodities. To collect statistics on sex roles I used the *Handbook of Latin American Studies* which includes indexes of archeological research articles for South America. From the *Handbook of Latin American Studies*, years 1976 through 1979, a sample of 401 South American contributors represents a male-to-female ratio of 1.7 to one. There are 1.7 times as many male archeologist authors as females. Compare this to North America: recent Ph.D.s from *Dissertation Abstracts* indicate a male:female ratio of 2:1, while NSF recipients show 7.8 times as many males as females receiving funds for these years. Numerically female archeologists are better represented in South American by both counts. On the other hand, perhaps comparing the dissertation writers or grant recipients with authors is not just, so I counted authors of articles and reports in *American Antiquity* for these years, excluding special topic issues. Male authors outnumber female authors by a ratio of 5:3.1 by this count. South American females are better represented in their archeological community than are North American women *by any count*.

What about sex-role assignments in South America? The South American samples, unlike more recent North American statistics, show almost identical distributions for male and female work: 78% of the males and 71% of the females report on field research, and collections analysis per se involves 22% of the males and 28% of the females. Compare with *American Antiquity*: 59% of the males and 19% of the females report on field research, and collections analysis involves 45% of the males and 81% of the females. The bulk of the reported archeological research in South America for both sexes is simply in the field . . . and women are in the field almost as much as men, and in considerably higher proportions than their North American counterparts.

The unexpected and even counter-intuitive results of this cross-cultural comparison are extremely informative. Most obviously they refute the argument that women are actually less qualified (or capable) of undertaking fieldwork leadership . . . that they are not tough enough, or, more subtly, that they haven't received appropriate training or encouragement to have learned to perform these tasks adequately. If South American women are in the field more than their North American counterparts it is neither being tougher nor having had more appropriate childhood training that has put them there.

A better explanation admits the anthropological insight that the categories by which a society groups its members are always culturally determined. "Sex is sex," says Gayle Rubin, "but what counts as sex is culturally determined . . . gender identity itself is a social product" (Rubin 1975:165–166). The apparently more equal role of the South American female archeologist may be related, at least in part, to the dominant, highly demarcated class system of Latin American society. In contrast to the North American ideology, which firmly denies the existence of a functioning class system, South Americans recognize and draw social divisions across lines of economic status, so that it is within class boundaries that gender plays a relative role in Latin society. Within the class of university-trained professionals South American women may be relatively free of gender restraints, being elites first and women second.

A number of alternative or complementary explanations are also possible. In countries where academic studies in general, and archeology in particular, are not highly valued, and admission into academic disciplines like archeology is not very competitive, women may be excluded less systematically. In contrast, where entry into academic disciplines (including archeology) is highly competitive, women may find it more difficult to participate in making meaningful contributions to knowledge. Very significantly, the traditional extended family operates as a support system to aid the female in Latin American society, providing her with childcare, assisting with household chores and offering moral and sometimes financial support (Erika Wagner, personal communication, 1985). Finally it is very probable that South American archeology is simply in an earlier phase of professional development and growth than is North American archeology, and that there is overall less job specialization among South American archeologists, suggesting that all South American practitioners are involved more or less in a similar range of tasks using similar methodological tools.

In this case we can expect South American women archeologists to become more marginalized out of their field research roles in the future, as archeology in their countries becomes more sociologically complex.

THE REPRODUCTION OF WOMEN-AT-HOME

Whatever combination of these factors is operating it is clear that within North American society archeological jobs are assigned according to gender. In order to create good matches between job and gender, work tasks come to be defined by particular and somewhat arbitrary characteristics which exaggerate their "masculine" or "feminine" aspects, intensifying recruitment from either one sex or the other. The inherently sex-neutral jobs of preliminary data collection come to be seen as "male." Naturally, then, as a specific job is occupied by more and more workers of one sex, there is a further increase in the gender loading of what the job entails. Men *make* the job male.

Thus fieldwork represents stereotypic male behavior, and women's access to it is blocked by a male-dominated sociological network. Grant-getting and professional advancement are clearly related to the endless oiling of collegial wheels, the bar-room banter, the politicking that underlies all professional networks, and power is disseminated from a male élite through the familiar old-boy network, teacher to student, colleague to colleague, based at least as much on sociological and social factors as on merit alone. The accumulation of advantage to males in this process is inevitable and has been noted in other scientific arenas. "Although women have moved *into* the community of science, they are not *of* that community . . . Many women continue to be excluded from the very activities that allow for full participation and growth, or productivity and change. These are, by and large, the informal activities of science — the heated discussion and debates, inclusion in the inner core or the invisible college, full participation in the social networks where scientists air ideas and generate new ones" (Cole 1981:389).

The net effect is that a male-defined and male-defended activity has been elevated to the rank of sacred archeological ritual, garnering two-thirds of the research funds and displacing women out of the production process and into the feminine backwater of analysis where funds are few and prestige is low. Armed with a new consciousness about the biases operating against women in the field women should be seeking to identify and combat the yet-unspecified factors that exclude them from field research, showing that they are not afraid to take on large responsibilities, go after the Big Money, and run major fieldwork projects.

But at the same time striving for validation via fieldwork is clearly at best a limited strategy for equilibrating women's status in archeology. The larger view adamantly reasserts that analytic research, in contrast to fieldwork, offers a more direct, more insightful, less costly and longer-sighted route to understanding the human past through social science methods. Philosophically it is a water-tight case. We will learn more by studying data from informed theoretical perspectives than by digging more holes in the ground. Practically speaking it is inevitable that, as museum collections come to outnumber remaining archeological sites in increasing proportions, priorities will have to shift to encourage original studies of prehistoric materials. The aggressive realignment of archeological roles and rewards to fit our anthropological goals must be the course of action for our discipline.

Ironically, women, already in an analytic ghetto, may be in the best position to spearhead this new direction, providing the guidance and the opportunities for archeology to mature into the social science it claims to be. But it is imperative that women only take on the challenge as equals, refusing second-class citizenship for doing high-priority research.

REFERENCES

Cole, Jonathan R. 1981. Women in Science. *American Scientist,* **69**, 385–391.

Conkey, Margaret L. 1978. Participation in the Research Process: Getting Grants. Paper presented at the 77th annual meeting of AAA, Los Angeles.

Conkey, Margaret W. 1982. Archeological Research, Gender Paradigms and Invisible Behavior. Paper presented at the 81st annual meeting of the AAA, Washington D.C.

Conkey, Margaret, L., and Spector, Janet D. 1984. Archeology and the study of gender. *Advances in Archeological Method and Theory Vol. 7.* Michael B. Schiffer, ed. pp. 1–38. New York: Academic Press.

Gero, Joan M. 1983. Gender Bias in Archeology: A Cross Cultural Perspective. *The Socio-Politics of Archeology.* J. M. Gero, D. Lacy, and M. L. Blakey, eds. pp. 51–57. Amherst: University of Massachusetts Department of Anthropology Research Report Number 23.

Gero, Joan M. 1985. Socio-politics of archeology and the woman-at-home ideology. *American Antiquity,* **50**, 342–350.

Kelley, Jane H., and Hanen, Marsha P. *Archeology and the Methodology of Science.* Albuquerque: University of New Mexico Press. In Press.

Rubin, Gayle. 1975. The Traffic in Women: Notes on the Political Economy of Sex. *Toward an Anthropology of Women.* Rayna Reiter, ed. pp. 157–210. New York: Monthly Review Press.

Winters, Howard D. 1968. Value Systems and Trade Cycles of the Late Archaic in the Midwest. *New Perspectives in Archeology,* Sally R. Binford and Lewis R. Binford, eds. pp. 175–221. Chicago: Aldine Publishing Co.

Woodall, J. Ned, and Perricone, Philip J. 1981. The Archeologist as Cowboy: the Consequence of Professional Stereotype. *Journal of Field Archeology,* **8**, 506–508.

Yellen, John. 1983. Women, Archeology and the National Science Foundation. *The Socio-politics of Archeology.* J. M. Gero, D. Lacy, and M. L. Blakey, eds. pp. 59–65. Amherst, Massachusetts: University of Massachusetts Department of Anthropology Research Report No. 23.

Chapter 3

Women in Public Health: Changes in a Profession

Jennie J. Kronenfeld

Despite recent increases in numbers of women entering as students and participating as professionals in various scientific fields and in the health professions women still lag behind men in many important areas. This includes not only numbers relative to their representation in the total population, but also salaries and unemployment rates in many scientific fields (Vetter 1981). In academic fields women lag behind in salaries, in rates of promotion through the academic ranks, and in recognition in scholarly communities, often despite similar qualifications, experience, and evaluations of job performance (Cole 1981; Levy 1985; Astin and Bayer 1973; Patterson 1973; Bernard 1984; Astin and Davis 1985).

Between 1950 and 1970 there were two divergent trends occurring in the representation of women as professionals in the labor force. In the 1950s the percentage of female professional workers actually dropped slightly and the percentage growth of female professionals lagged behind that of males even in traditionally female professions such as school teacher, librarian or social worker (U.S. Bureau of the Census 1960). These trends began to reverse in the 1960s and changed in major ways by 1980, particularly in terms of enrollment of women in professional schools in traditionally male fields such as law and medicine. While fewer studies have focused on a field such as public health there have been two studies which have explicitly examined the role of women in the last 20 years (Yokopenic et al. 1975; Levy 1985). Both focused upon data on participation in certain kinds of activities in the largest overall professional association in the field, the American Public Health Association (APHA). This chapter will build upon those two previous studies and will examine first the situation of women as practicing public health professionals. This portion of the chapter will emphasize data on participation in the professional association using previously collected data plus some data on participation in the annual meeting in 1986. Some limited information on salary ranges in subfields will also be discussed. The chapter will then focus upon the role of women as students and faculty in schools of public health. This is important both for understanding the current status of women in the field and for projecting the kinds of changes which may occur in the next 10 to 15 years, based on current trends among students.

THE FIELD OF PUBLIC HEALTH

Unlike traditional scientific disciplines, the field of public health is multidisciplinary. It includes the full range of medical specialities, each of the social sciences, some aspect of engineering, business, nursing, education, and numerous clinical specialties. At its core are disciplines such as epidemiology (the study of the distribution and causes of diseases in populations) and biostatistics (the application of statistical techniques and thought to human populations and to health of those populations). While the 23 accredited schools of public health do not all have the same number and names of academic departments, there are nine basic specialties around which many of the larger schools are organized. Some smaller schools have only a subset of these fields of study available. The fields are: biostatistics, epidemiology, health services administration, public health practice and program management (often subsumed under health administration and including other health professional specializations as applied to public health such as dental public health, public health nursing, public health social work, etc.), health education, environmental health sciences, occupational safety and health, nutrition, and biomedical and laboratory sciences (such as microbiology and parasitology). Other areas covered by some schools include international health, population/ family planning, and genetics.

Public health as a field of study in the United States dates back to the first decades of the twentieth century. Schools of public health often had their beginnings in university schools of medicine but then were created as separate schools. The two earliest were those at Johns Hopkins University and Harvard University. The professional association, APHA, first met in 1873. The official publication of APHA, the *American Journal of Public Health*, published its first issue in 1911 and has remained in continuous publication since that time. The numbers of schools of public health remained small throughout the decades of the 1920s and 1930s. Many of the early practitioners were already trained as health professionals (especially as physicians and nurses) in the early decades of the century. Since that time the field has experienced several major periods of growth. One such period occurred after World War II when a number of new state-supported schools of public health were created. Also at this time more diverse groups of students were attracted into careers as public health professionals, and studies of health care delivery, health education, social factors in health, and chronic diseases expanded the boundary of concerns of public health as a field. Another period of growth started in the late 1960s and continued into the 1970s with more new schools being created and further expansion of concerns about the organization of health care delivery, the environment, and family planning as well as other diverse areas.

This increasing diversity of areas of study and knowledge presents interesting questions of how to approach the field and also interesting findings as contrasted with studies of one specific scientific discipline. One unusual aspect of using public health as a field in which to study changes in women's labor force participation and participation in professions (versus more traditional disciplinary-based fields in science) is that the great diversity of subject matter covered by public health means the field has always included some areas that were heavily and traditionally female (such as public health nursing) as well as areas that were heavily and traditionally male (environmental health, health administration, epidemiology, biostatistics). Women's participation in public health has been increasing greatly in the last decade, almost to the point that some subfields are being increasingly "feminized" in a numerical sense, that is, they are being dominated by the presence of large numbers of women. The percentage of women graduating from schools of public health went from 46 in the academic year 1974–75 to almost 60 in 1981–82 (Levy 1985). Estimates of increased participation by women in activities of APHA demonstrate a similar although less dramatic trend: increases from 41% of the membership being women in 1973 to 48% in 1983. This is during the same period of time when numbers and percentages of women entering other health care professions such as medicine and dentistry have also increased (U.S. Department of Health and Human Services 1984). The role of women in public health will be examined first by reviewing the role of women in APHA, and then by reviewing the role of women in schools of public health, both as students and as faculty.

WOMEN AS PUBLIC HEALTH PRACTITIONERS — THE ROLE OF WOMEN IN APHA

Many sociologists of science and the professions have pointed out that professions operate as communities within larger societies (Goode 1957; Epstein 1970; Hagstrom 1965). An important part of the way a profession operates is that it produces the next generation socially through its control over the selection of professional trainees and through the roles of informal and formal channels of communication that help to increase individual visibility. This visibility outside the immediate job of an individual becomes an important sign of external recognition which then becomes crucial to both vertical and horizontal mobility within a profession.

Important ways in which this visibility occurs in professions are through presentations of papers at professional meetings and membership on committees and in leadership roles (either elected or appointed) of professional associations. Often recognition by the professional association in such roles may become an important factor in eligibility for promotion within the work environment. In the past, both in professions and in the sciences, there is evidence that such collegial circles have been less open to women than to men and that the lack of inclusion in these professional networks has hindered the advancement of women (Bernard 1984; Hagstrom 1965). Bernard has described this as a "stag effect." Both of the previous studies of the role of women in public health have started from the premise that participation in the communication networks of a professional community both reflects and helps later to predict career mobility and occupational achievement (Levy 1985; Yokopenic et al. 1975). Given this assumption and the dearth of available data on participation rates of women as public health practitioners at local, state, or national levels both at the times those two studies were done and currently, studies of women as practitioners have focused on the role of women in the public health professional association, APHA.

A similar methodology to study this issue was used in the 1975 and 1985 studies and was extended to 1986 by this author. Yokopenic and colleagues (1975) performed a content analysis of the official printed program from the 1973 annual meeting of the American Public Health Association. Four areas of activity were examined:

1. membership on governing bodies;

2. total participation by women in the official program including such roles as chairing sessions and memberships in panels;

3. submission of female-authored abstracts;

4. presentation of female-authored papers.

Sex was recorded as male, female, or unknown (which occurred in cases where first names were ambiguous or initials were used). A paper or abstract was coded as female if at least one of the authors was a woman, thus inflating to some extent the participation figures of women. Levy (1985) adopted a very similar methodology to analyze the printed program of the 1983 APHA meeting. She examined three of the four categories used by the earlier study; submission of abstracts was not examined due to lack of data. Given the recent date of this analysis a more limited examination of the 1986 APHA printed program was conducted for this paper. Figures were tabulated on governing positions, presiders for each session, and participants in each session.

The Levy (1985) paper also contains information on membership in the various sections of APHA by sex for 1983. Such information was not available in 1973 or 1986. This is very important information for looking at participation in the program for 1985, and thus the 1983 membership figures are reported in Table 3.1. Between 1973 and 1983 the number of women in APHA increased by 7%, up to 48.2% of the membership being female by 1983. Estimates based on continued increases in female enrollment in schools of public health during this 3-year period indicate that female membership in APHA has probably continued to increase and the 1986 membership is probably now at or over 50% female. There were some changes in the numbers of sections between 1973 and 1983 and

TABLE 3.1. *Total Number of APHA Members by Sex and Section, 1983*

Section	Number of Section Members	Number of Women	Percentage of Women
Community Health Planning	1130	649	48.8
Dental Health	634	192	30.8
Environment	1001	122	12.2
Epidemiology	1932	672	34.8
Food and Nutrition	1111	864	77.8
Gerontological Health	787	493	62.6
Health Administration	3781	1350	35.7
International Health	1123	451	40.2
Injury Control and Emergency Health Services	–	–	–
Laboratory	616	182	29.5
Maternal and Child Health	1711	1107	64.7
Medical Care	2270	686	30.2
Mental Health	930	384	41.3
New Professionals	187	118	63.1
Occupational Health and Safety	1020	347	34.0
Podiatric	493	21	4.3
Population and Family Planning	628	374	59.6
Public Health Education	2133	1410	66.1
Public Health Nursing	2780	2716	97.7
Radiological Health	381	47	12.3
School Health	399	245	61.4
Social Work	413	316	76.5
Statistics	641	242	37.8
Veterinary Public Health	195	19	9.7
Vision Care	619	56	9.0
Total	27,155	13,063	48.2%

Source: Levy, Judith. "Women's Status in the Professions: The APHA Revisited," Presented at 1985 APHA Meeting.

further changes in 1986. One section, Injury Control and Emergency Services, was no longer a section but rather a special interest group by 1983. Four new sections were formed: gerontological health, international health, population and family planning, and vision care. By 1986 the new professions section had disbanded, as had veterinary health, while one new section, alcohol and drugs, was created. While the overall membership of APHA is half female, section membership varies greatly from a low of 4% female in the podiatric health (chiropody) section to a high of almost 98% female in the public health nursing section. This table makes very clear the continued presence of traditional sex-based distinctions with partici-pation in the subfields of public health. In addition to nursing other groups that include either traditional women's fields or areas of special interest to women are those with the highest female memberships, including food and nutrition (77.8%), social work (76.5%), public health education (66.1%), maternal and child health (64.7%), and school health (61.4%). Two other sections with over 60% female membership are new professionals (63.1%) and gerontological health (62.6%). Besides podiatric health, four other sections had less than 15% female membership. These included the traditionally male-dominated professions of veterinary public health (9.7%), vision care (9%), and radiological health (12.3%) along with environmental health (12.2%), a longstanding male-dominated field within public health.

What is the participation of women in governing roles within the American Public Health Association? Women have increased their participation in overall governing roles, both from 1973 to 1983 and to a lesser extent to 1986. In 1973 only 25% of people in the governing roles shown in Table 3.2 were female. This increased greatly, up to 38% in 1983 and somewhat more, to 42% by 1986, although these figures for 1983 and 1986 are probably still somewhat below the representation of females in the overall membership of the association. Women's role as leaders of sections during this time changed from 5 of 21 in 1973 to 6 of 24 in 1983. A large increase occurred by 1985 with 10 of 23 sections chaired by women. The earlier papers by Yokopenic and colleagues (1975) and Levy (1985) also examined in greater detail the role of women as leaders in sections. In 1973 women were quite under-represented in section councils. Even in sections in which in 1973 women made up roughly half of the members, such as Medical Care and Mental Health, they generally represented only 20% to 30% of the leadership positions. Only in the overwhelmingly female sections such as public health nursing and school health did women represent the majority or, in the case of nursing, all of the leadership. By 1983, while five sections still had no women representatives and few women council members, most sections showed positive gains for women.

Participation of women in the program at APHA has increased greatly since 1973. At that time Yokopenic and colleagues (1975) found women

TABLE 3.2. *Number and Percentage of Women in Non-Section APHA Governing Groups, 1973, 1983, and 1985*

Governing Group	Gender 1973			Gender 1983			Gender 1986		
	W	U	T	W	U	T	W	U	T
Governing Body									
Members									
Officers	1	0	10	3	0	10	2	0	10
Executive Board	4	0	12	6	0	12	5	0	12
Board Chair	0	0	2	1	0	3	0	0	2
Chair of Steering									
Committees	2	0	6	2	0	4	2	0	4
Chair of Sections	5	0	21	6	0	24	10	0	23
Representation of Affiliated Association and Regional Boards	14	4	53	20	1	47	23	1	48
Total	26	4	104	38	1	100	42	1	99
Percent	25%	3.8%		38%	1%		42%	1%	

W = Women   U = Unknown Sex   T = Total

concentrated in participation in the program activities of those sections in which they made up a large proportion of the members. In other sections women were frequently 10% to 20% of the program participants (see Table 3.3), although no or less than 5% of the program participants were female in sections such as environmental, podiatric, radiological, and veterinary. The 1973 data also included information on numbers of abstracts submitted and acceptance rates. In 1973 abstracts by women were less likely to be selected for presentation and this appeared particularly true in the case of single-authored abstracts.

By 1983 participation rates of women in the program had increased in almost all sections, with the exception of a decrease in female dominance in a section such as public health nursing. In only four sections (environmental, laboratory, podiatric, and veterinary public health) were there 30% or fewer papers with women listed as authors or participating in some way in the session (as session organizers or discussants, for example). In some sections, however, participation rates by women were still below the percentage of the section membership that was female. By 1986 the participation of women in the program in most sections had increased even further. One explanation for this is an increase in the number of multi-authored papers. Following the approach used by the previous authors on this topic, a presentation in which any one of the authors could be identified as a woman was counted as participation by a woman in that event, thus to some extent inflating the figures on participation by women

TABLE 3.3. *Participation of Women in APHA Program, by Section, 1973, 1983, 1986*

Section	1973 % Women	1973 % Unknown	1983 % Women	1983 % Unknown	1986 % Women	1986 % Unknown
Alcohol and Drug	–	–	–	–	48.5	5.9
Community Health Planning	12.1	4.4	34.5	4.0	48.0	4.0
Dental Health	12.7	8.5	38.7	1.7	60.0	0.0
Environmental	2.5	6.2	21.7	9.5	51.7	10.3
Epidemiology	12.0	11.0	30.5	8.9	47.1	2.8
Food and Nutrition	43.2	15.9	42.5	5.1	85.9	0.0
Gerontological Health	–	–	47.6	5.5	56.8	1.8
Health Administration	15.6	4.4	39.3	2.4	51.0	0.5
International Health	–	–	34.2	6.2	48.3	0.0
Injury Control	18.8	10.9	–	–	–	–
Laboratory	12.6	10.8	29.4	6.0	40.0	2.5
Maternal and Child Health	31.5	7.7	52.6	4.5	73.6	0.6
Medical Care	20.2	4.7	31.5	3.0	44.8	1.1
Mental Health	10.9	6.5	36.4	3.6	55.5	0.0
New Professionals	30.3	3.0	36.5	2.9	–	–
Occupational Health	24.1	10.3	36.2	2.4	53.1	2.3
Podiatric	0.0	0.0	26.7	0.0	9.1	0.0
Population and Family Planning	–	–	50.4	8.8	73.2	0.0
Public Health Education	50.0	11.5	53.6	2.9	65.5	0.7
Public Health Nursing	75.6	4.9	55.7	4.2	94.8	0.9
Radiological Health	0.0	0.0	30.4	5.4	11.1	7.4
School Health	36.6	4.2	54.8	0.7	71.8	0.0
Social Work	42.1	10.5	59.4	2.1	84.3	0.0
Statistics	17.0	12.8	30.1	8.7	37.0	0.0
Veterinary Public Health	0.0	20.0	18.5	7.4	–	–
Vision Care	–	–	43.6	7.2	27.6	3.6

Source: Magee 1986.

as compared, for example, with the actual number of female presenters on a panel of speakers at any one point in time. While separate statistics on female authorships depending on numbers of authors were not gathered in 1976 they were in 1983. The largest increase from 1973 to 1983 occurred in co-authored papers (Levy 1985). About 44% of single-authored papers were by a woman in 1983, whereas 73% of papers by three or more authors included at least one woman in 1983.

One further way to examine participation by women in the activities of the association is to look at a more specific role, that of chairing sessions at the annual meeting. Table 3.4 contains information on participation by sex by section in 1986 as chairpersons of sessions. In contrast to total participation in the program where participation figures by females are inflated due to the large numbers of papers that are multi-authored, this is not true for being asked to chair a session. Also, depending on the policies

TABLE 3.4. *Participation of Women in APHA Programs, as Presiders, by Section, 1986*

Section	% Women	% Unknown
Alcohol and Drug	18.2	27.3
Community Health Planning	36.4	9.1
Dental Health	63.6	0.0
Environment	15.4	23.1
Epidemiology	28.6	14.3
Food and Nutrition	91.7	0.0
Gerontological Health	38.1	4.8
Health Administration	53.2	2.1
International Health	50.0	0.0
Laboratory	33.3	16.7
Maternal and Child Health	69.2	3.8
Medical Care	36.1	5.5
Mental Health	55.5	0.0
Occupational Health	42.3	11.5
Podiatric Health	0.0	0.0
Population	73.0	0.0
Public Health Education	57.7	3.8
Public Health Nursing	87.0	4.3
Radiological	0.0	33.3
School Health	76.9	0.0
Social Work	66.7	0.0
Statistics	21.1	0.0
Vision Care	0.0	14.3

of each section, a large amount of program participation is determined competitively through selection of abstracts and, in some sections, this is conducted through a blind process (the names of all authors are deleted from the abstract during the selection process). Being asked to chair a section may be a better indicator of participation in informal activities than the competitive selection of abstracts. It is in these informal activities that some studies of the development of colleague networks in science find discrimination against women persisting the longest. The percentage of participation by women as session chairpersons does vary more by section (a range of 0% to 92%) than does any participation in the program. In general, sections with high female membership are those where females are most likely to chair sections, and the sections in which there are no female chairs (podiatric, radiological, vision care) are the most male dominated. In most sessions participation by women in the program in general and participation as session chairs are similar. In a few sections, particularly environmental health and epidemiology, almost half of all program participants are female but only 15% and 29% of sessions chairpersons are, perhaps reflecting recent growth of female participation in these areas, a trend which can be examined more clearly with data on trends in enrollments in schools of public health.

One last aspect of potential discrimination against women as current public health professionals is the thorny issue of salary. In many fields, salary differentials either between men and women professionals or across predominantly male versus female job categories have been found to be among the last areas of change (Bernard 1984; Kashket et al. 1974; Schiller 1969; Sutter and Miller 1973). Salary information also tends to be very difficult to obtain. While the American Public Health Association has not conducted salary studies examining differences in pay by sex, they did conduct a study in 1982 of employee compensation in local health departments. This study examined various job classifications (American Public Health Association 1984). Given what is generally known about sex distribution in subfields of practice in public health, this information provides a brief examination of partially sex-based differences in pay in public health. The three most useful classifications to compare are health administrators (in 1982 still a predominantly male field), public health nurses (an overwhelmingly female field) and health educators (a dispro-portionately female field, but much less so than nursing). In all three areas the desired education for professionals would be a master's degree and a minimum education would generally be a bachelor's degree. Thus differences in educational requirements of the field should not play a role in explaining income differentials. The median income for health adminis-trators (non-physician) was $26,000 with a maximum of $60,000. For health educators the median was $18,000 with a $39,000 maximum and for public health nurses the median was $16,000 and the maximum was

$28,000. These figures indicated that sex-based differentials in pay exist in public health as in many other fields.

WOMEN IN SCHOOLS OF PUBLIC HEALTH

Over the last 25 years one ongoing trend in schools of public health is an increase in the representation of women. Whereas the typical student in public health in 1960 was a white male, often with a medical background, it is much less possible to describe a typical student by the mid 1980s. That student is far more likely now to be female, to be older, more experienced and currently working and attending school on a part-time basis. In 1960–61 only 28% of the student body was female. The proportion of women has steadily increased, to 46% in 1974 and up to almost 60% in 1984. Thus the very character of public health as a field is undergoing major shifts (at least in terms of current students) from a traditionally male field with a few large female subfields to a slightly predominantly female field with traditionally female subfields remaining so and some predominantly male strongholds remaining so, but to a lesser extent than in the past. These changes and increased representation of women are less true in terms of female representation on faculties of schools of public health. This section will first describe the status of women as applicants, new enrollees, students, and graduates of schools of public health and then examine the role of women as faculty.

WOMEN AS STUDENTS

One initial way to examine students and their participation in public health is to look at available statistics on the applicant pool. In 1974, 43% of applicants were female. This increased to 60% by 1984. More interesting than overall data on the applicant pool is information by area of specialization. Table 3.5 presents information on the area of specialization of new enrollments in schools of public health in 1984. In all of the tables reporting data from schools of public health, many fewer areas of specialization are included than in the lists of sections of the APHA, due to differences in the records systems for the schools versus the professional association. This lessened number of categories will diminish the ability to examine certain trends, particularly since the category of public health practice and program management includes together such areas as public health nursing, maternal and child health, dental public health, geron-tology, and mental health. Thus some of the areas most dominated traditionally by women are mixed in with more diverse areas. It does reflect major trends within schools of public health, however, in which separate departments in these categories tend to be less common now than in 1970. The categories used in the tables reflect the more typical

TABLE 3.5. *New Enrollments in Schools of Public Health by Area by Sex, 1984*

Area	% Female	Total Enrollment
Biostatistics	54.9	137.5
Epidemiology	55.4	445.0
Health Services Administration	62.6	998.5
Public Health Practice and Program Management	72.6	308.5
Health Education/Behavioral Science	74.7	326.5
Environmental Science	39.9	422.0
Occupational Safety and Health	48.9	48.0
Nutrition	86.8	144.5
Biomedical and Laboratory Sciences	52.7	110.0
Other	64.0	302.5

Source: Magee 1986.

departments within large schools of public health (in some smaller schools fewer departments are included).

Women in 1984 range from being 40% of the new enrollees in a traditionally male-dominated area such as environmental health sciences to 87% of the new enrollees in nutrition. Besides environmental, women represent less than half of the new enrollees in only one area, occupational safety and health (49%). The large role of women in a field such as public health nursing is diminished in the combined category of public health practice and program management so that women comprise 73% of this area. Health education and behavioral sciences is another area in which three-quarters of new students are female. While area of study is the most important factor explaining differences in enrollment of women students there is also variability by school of public health. On the low end, women comprise only 44% and 48% of new students at Tulane University in Louisiana and Loma Linda in California. On the high end, three-quarters of the new enrollment is female at many schools including Yale, Harvard, Boston University, and University of California at Berkeley.

Table 3.6 presents trends in female enrollment by area of specialization for four different time periods from 1974 through 1984. In all fields the female percentage has increased since 1974–75, although in the most female-dominated field (nutrition) the increase has been small (from 80.6% in 1974–75 to 83.5% in 1984). In 1974 the three most male-dominated fields were occupational safety and health (only 17% female), environmental sciences (27%) and biostatistics (38%). By 1984 a slight majority (53%) of biostatistics students are female. Environmental has increased to 40% and one-third of occupational health students are female. Fields such as health education went from being half female to three-

TABLE 3.6. *Percent of Students in Schools of Public Health, Female, by Area of Study, by Sex, 1974–75, 1978–79, 1981, 1984*

Area	1974–75	1978–79	1981	1984
Biostatistics	37.9	45.8	48.4	53.1
Epidemiology	43.6	45.7	54.0	58.8
Health Services Administration	41.4	50.2	58.6	61.9
Public Health Practice and Program Management	60.1	72.2	66.8	74.7
Health Education/Behavioral Science	48.5	66.1	73.6	74.1
Environmental Science	26.8	30.9	40.3	40.0
Occupational Safety and Health	17.5	32.3	31.1	33.5
Nutrition	80.6	80.4	85.3	83.5
Biomedical and Laboratory Sciences	–*	41.8	42.9	52.0
Other	–*	50.5	52.8	59.5

* = not comparable for 1974–75.

quarters female and a traditionally male field such as health administration has 62% female enrollment by 1984.

Beyond the area of specialization the increased numbers of female students may impact on other changes in public health. In 1984, 24% of males are enrolled in doctoral programs while only 19% of female students are in doctoral programs, although the vast majority of both groups are in master's programs. Female students as a group have less prior education than male students. For U.S. women in 1981–82, 72% had a bachelor's degree as their highest previous degree versus 56% of men. Only 3% of women students had health practitioner doctorates (M.D., D.D.S., D.V.M.) versus 14% of males.

The group most likely to impact upon the future composition of all public health practitioners consists of those students who actually graduate from schools of public health. The pattern of increasing female dominance is true for graduates as for applicants, new enrollees and current students. In 1960 only 28% of graduates were female and this dropped as low as 23% in one year in the 1960s. By 1974–75, 44% of graduates were female. Roughly half of graduates were female for the first time in 1977–78. This increased to 59% by 1984–85. In terms of impact on the field of practice the new graduates will have a large statistical impact, since there were only 770 graduates of schools of public health in 1960–61 versus over 3,000 graduates annually by 1980–81.

Table 3.7 presents figures on the percentage of graduates of schools of public health that are female by area of study for 1982, 1983, and 1984. The figures are quite similar to those in Tables 3.5 and 3.6. The smallest percentage of female graduates is in occupational health (about 30%). In

TABLE 3.7. *Percent of Graduates of Schools of Public Health, Female, by Area of Study, by Sex, 1982, 1983, 1984*

Area of Study		% Female	
	1982	1983	1984
Biostatistics	57.9	52.8	58.5
Epidemiology	51.6	48.2	51.2
Health Services Administration	56.6	57.4	62.9
Public Health Practice and Program Management	70.6	74.5	74.8
Health Education and Behavior Science	70.2	75.4	76.7
Environmental Sciences	38.5	39.9	39.2
Occupational Safety and Health	32.7	31.7	29.9
Nutrition	85.5	81.7	78.7
Biomedical and Laboratory Science	48.6	44.4	48.6
Other	52.1	50.3	55.4

this area the percentage of female graduates has declined slightly since 1982. Not quite 40% of environmental health sciences graduates are female. In all other fields about half or more of graduates are female. Women comprise three-quarters of graduates in nutrition, health education, and public health practice. In one area, occupational health sciences, figures on new enrollees for 1984 (49% from Table 3.5) may indicate a substantial increase in female graduates in the future.

The increased enrollment of female students has implications for the practitioner mix in future years. The large number of current graduates each year and the steady dominance of female students beginning in the late 1970s will change the proportion of females in the overall field by the year 2000. Not only will public health by then be a predominantly female profession if current trends continue, but even the traditionally male-dominated fields will have a substantial proportion of females.

WOMEN AS FACULTY

These trends of increasing proportions of women in most fields and of female dominance in actual numbers of students in schools of public health are not true if one examines trend data on women as faculty members in schools of public health. Faculty positions can be considered to represent one type of élite in the field. Another type of élite would be state health commissioners and those in other leading practice-oriented positions in public health. In both types of élite positions women have not yet attained equity with men, despite dominance in starting roles (that is as students).

Table 3.8 contains information on the percentage of faculty that are female for three time periods, from 1976–77 through 1984–85, by area of specialization. Overall the proportion of the faculty which is female has not changed substantially (from 27% in 1976–77 to 25% in 1984–85). The largest area for female faculty in 1976–77 was in public health practice and program management (79 faculty or 18% of all women faculty) and health education-behavioral science, followed closely by epidemiology. Trends are similar for 1980–81. By 1984–85 there is a decrease in the relative concentration of women faculty in fields such as health education, public health practice, and epidemiology and an increase in the proportion of women faculty who teach in the areas of environmental sciences and health services administration.

Table 3.9 includes information on the percentage of faculty by sex in each area of specialization. These figures can be compared with the proportion of female students and graduates in each area in the same time

TABLE 3.8. *Female Faculty in U.S. Schools of Public Health by Areas of Specialization*

Area	1976–77		1980–81		1984–85	
		%		%		%
Biostatistics	47	10.9%	36	9.8%	45	10.5%
Epidemiology	72	16.6	53	14.4	61	14.2
Health Services Administration	61	14.1	49	13.3	73	17.0
Public Health Practice and Program Management	79	18.2	60	16.3	63	14.7
Health Education/ Behavioral Sciences	78	18.0	31	8.4	62	14.5
Environmental Sciences	19	4.3	9	2.4	25	5.8
OS and H	8	1.8	12	3.3	2	0.5
Nutrition	34	7.9	31	8.4[†]	39	9.1
Biomedical and Laboratory Science	N/A	–	15	4.1	22	5.1
Other Areas	35	8.1	73	19.8	37	8.6
Unknown	36	–	49	–	–	–
TOTAL	469	100.0	418	100.0	429	100.0
TOTAL FACULTY	1752		1644		1680	
* % FEMALE		27.4		25.8		25.5

* % Calculated without unknowns.
† Behavioral sciences not included — that accounts for the difference. B.S. students in other areas.

TABLE 3.9. *Percentage of Faculty that is Female in Areas of Speciality, 1976–77 and 1980–81*

Area	% of Faculty that is Female	
	1976–77	1980–81
Biostatistics	28.0	18.8
Epidemiology	23.0	30.3
Health Services Administration	21.2	20.7
Public Health Practice and Program Management	47.6	53.6
Health Education*	41.2	43.7
Environmental Sciences	8.5	6.4
Occupational Health Safety	17.4	15.8
Nutrition	48.6	41.3
Biomedical and Laboratory Science	–	16.3
Other Areas	19.6	23.6
Unknown	29.7	29.9

* Behavioral Sciences is in Health Education, 1976–77 and in other, 1980–81.

frame in the earlier tables. In only one area, public health practice and management, do women comprise half of the faculty as contrasted with women comprising over half of the student body in a majority of the areas of specialization. In several of the areas the representation of women actually decreased over the 4-year period in the table, although there are too few data points available to demonstrate a clear trend. This is true in biostatistics (28% female the first period versus 19% in 1980–81), nutrition (48.6% to 41.3%) and to a lesser extent in environmental health sciences and occupational health. In those two areas less than 10% and 20% of the faculty are female respectively at either point in time. Nutrition is a heavily female-dominated field in terms of enrollment and as reflected by membership in the appropriate section of APHA. Relative to those figures women are under-represented in faculty positions and their proportion is decreasing.

One of the major roles of university faculty is to conduct research and publish the results of this research. While the representation of women on the faculties of schools of public health has not improved in the last 10 years, the first part of this paper illustrated that women are becoming better represented in overall leadership roles in the professional association, APHA, and in presentations at meetings. What has been the representation of women in written publications? A cursory examination of this is available from an article reviewing the 75-year history of the official general journal of the association, the *American Journal of Public Health* (Yankauer 1986). One question is whether the journal represents the practitioner or academic community in terms of authorship. This has changed greatly over the years. Until 1970 most authors of articles were government employees in contrast to university officials. By 1980 university faculty members were two-thirds of the primary authors of published papers. Women were rarely authors through the 1930s (only 3%, mostly nurses or laboratory workers). By 1970, 20% of the primary authors were female and this increased to 30% in 1980, a figure somewhat higher than the percentage of female faculty in schools of public health. These data indicate adequate representation of women as published authors in the main general journal in the field.

SUMMARY

What has been the response of public health as a field to the increasing participation of women in the labor force in general and in professional fields in particular? As judged by numbers alone (whether as students or in sections of the professional association), public health has been open to increased participation of women. In fact women are now the majority group in the student population and close to that in the professional association. Given the dominance of women as students the role of women numerically in the professional association should continue to increase to the year 2000. There remains diversity by subfield, and these overall trends do not hold for a few traditionally male-dominated areas, but even those areas are generally less male dominated now than in the past.

Beyond numbers the role of women in the professional association as program participants and as section leaders is increasing. While it may not yet have increased as rapidly as overall numbers, the trends are indicative of increased roles for women. Since leadership roles in associations usually occur after the initial years in the field, the representation of women in leadership roles is probably proportionate to their memberships in those age cohorts.

Areas in practice in which women appear to be disadvantaged relative to men are in the most visible national leadership positions (such as being the state health officer) and in pay. Visibility in top leadership roles should change over time, given the greatly increased numbers of women in the field. One caution in this regard is that many states require the state health officer to be a physician and women students in public health are less likely to be physicians than are men. To some extent this may hinder the ability of women to move into the most visible leadership roles in state health departments.

Pay differentials are a more difficult issue. The data available to this paper did not explicitly address pay discrimination by sex, but rather by type of job. Changing the pay of whole subfields (such as nursing) to make it comparable to other fields with similar levels of education is a thorny issue and involves the current argument of comparable worth as a way to reform pay, especially pay in structured state employment systems (Whicker and Kronenfeld 1986; Lorber and Kirk 1983; England and Norris 1985). The legal status of the comparable-worth argument is currently being debated in the courts. Its success may play a major role in addressing differentials in pay in public health. Another important way to study whether clear pay discrimination by sex exists in the future is to look at the new group of graduating public health students 10 to 20 years from now, particularly those in traditionally male and well-paid fields such as health administration. Will those female students have similar promotions and earnings by the year 2000?

The last aspect of achievements of women in public health is also a difficult one in which to evaluate progress and response: the representation of women on faculties of public health. As contrasted with student representation and representation in the association little or no change has occurred in the representation of women on faculties in schools of public health. Why might this be the case? One explanation is that women are less likely to be in the available employment pool from which faculty members are drawn. While among current students males are more likely to be in doctorate programs (and thus are potential for future faculty) than females, the disproportion is not that great. Faculties change their composition much more slowly than do student bodies; therefore change in female composition of the faculty should be slower. This could provide a partial explanation for slower increases among faculty than students, however no increase has occurred in the last eight years. It is important to realize that, unlike many disciplinary fields in which graduate enrollment in the discipline is the total labor pool from which faculty are then drawn, public health faculty do not all have degrees in public health. Many are drawn from social sciences, administration, education, or basic science programs. With the possible exception of basic sciences, however, female enrollment in these graduate programs has generally been increasing although not necessarily at the rate that it has within public health. In sum, available explanations do not appear to explain the lack of change in female representation in this area. Perhaps the time lag is greater for change here. Both in the area of faculty representation and pay an examination of trends by the year 2000 will provide a more complete picture of the responses of the field of public health to growing labor force participation and changing occupational roles of women. At present the visibility and status of women in public health have increased greatly, but pay and faculty representation lag behind both the numerical increases and the increasing diversity in the sub-fields of study in public health in which women are important.

REFERENCES

American Public Health Association. 1984. *Survey of Employee Compensation in Local Health Departments. United States – 1982.* Washington, D.C.

Astin, Helen S., and Bayer, Alan E. 1973. Sex Discrimination in Academe. Alice Rossi and Ann Calderwood eds. *Academic Women on the Move.* New York: The Russell Sage Foundation.

Astin, Helen S., and Davis, D. 1985. Research Productivity Across the Life and Career-Cycles: Facilitators and Barriers For Women.

Bernard, Jessie. 1984. *Academic Women.* University Park, Pa.: The Pennsylvanian State University Press.

Cole, J. R. 1981. Women in Science. *American Scientist,* **69**: 385–391.

England, Paula, and Norris, Banar. 1985. Comparable Worth: A New Doctrine of Sex Discrimination. *Social Science Quarterly,* **66** (September): 627–642.

Epstein, Cynthia. 1970. Encountering The Male Establishment: Sex Limits on Women's Careers in the Professions. *American Journal of Sociology.* **75**: 965–982.

Goode, William J. 1957. Community Within a Community. *American Sociological Review,* **22**: 194–200.

Hagstrom, W. O. 1965. *The Scientific Community.* New York: Basic Books.

Kashket, Eva Ruth, Robbins, Mary Louise, Leive, Loretta and Huang, Alice S. 1974. Status of Women Microbiologists. *Science,* **183** (February): 488–494.

Levy, Judith. 1985. Women's Status in the Professions: The American Public Health Association Revisited. American Public Health Association Annual Meeting, Washington, D.C.

Lorber, Lawrence Z., and Kirk, J. Robert. 1983. A Status Report on the Theory of Comparable Worth: Recent Developments in the Law of Wage Discrimination. *Public Personnel Management,* **12** (Winter): 332–344.

Magee, Judith H. 1986. *U.S. Schools of Public Health: Data Report on Applicants, Students, Graduates, and Expenditures, 1984–85.* Washington, D.C.: Association of Schools of Public Health.

Patterson, Michele, 1973. Sex and Specialization in Academe and the Professions. Alice Rossi and Ann Calderwood, eds. *Academic Women on the Move.* New York: The Russell Sage Foundation.

Schiller, Anita R. 1969. The Widening Sex Gap. *Library Journal,* **94**: 1098–1100.

Sutter, Larry, and Miller, Herman P. 1973. Income Differences Between Men and Career Women. *American Journal of Sociology,* **78**: 200–215.

U.S. Bureau of the Census. 1960. *Census of the Population, 1960.* PC(1)–1D, Detailed Characteristics. Washington, D.C.: U.S. Government Printing Office.

U.S. Department of Health and Human Services. 1984. *Minorities and Women in the Health Field.* DDHS Publication No. HRS–DV–84–85. Washington, D.C.: U.S. Government Printing Office.

Vetter, B. M. 1981. Women Scientists and Engineers: Trends in Participation. *Science,* **214** (81): 1313–1321.

Whicker, Marcia, and Kronenfeld, Jennie Jacobs. 1986. Comparable Worth: An Issue of the Eighties. *Public Affairs Bulletin.* Number 33 (June).

Yankauer, Alfred. 1986. The American Journal of Public Health, 1911–85. *American Journal of Public Health.* **76** (7): 809–815.

Yokopenic, Patricia, Bourque, Linda Brookover, and Brogan, Donna. 1975. Professional Communications Networks: A Case Study of Women in the American Public Health Association. *Social Problems,* **22** (4): 493–509.

Chapter 4

Contemporary Concerns of Women in Medicine

Joan M. Altekruse and
Suzanne W. McDermott

INTRODUCTION

The history of women in medicine, like that of women in general, has not been fully recorded. Sufficient information has been conserved to establish that women have contributed to medicine from mythologic times to the present. From earliest known history the stories of women in medicine have spanned the centuries and the routes of civilization: east to China, west to the Middle East, to the ancient and modern nations of Europe and across the transcontinental passages of the New World. Their roles, as herbalists, midwives and care givers to infants and aged, to the sick and the well, were predominantly in the interests of family and neighbors. Public roles earned historical mention only when they were inordinately visible, given women's inferior social status. Recognition of women engaged in medicine typically occurred because they were members of royal families and only secondarily in relation to their activities as practitioners. Barriers established by church, state and other institutions of culture conspired to support the alleged inferiority or deviancy of women who performed the healing arts. Punitive responses to female practitioners ranged from social and professional discrimination to public execution for witchcraft.

As more rigorous bases for medical practice developed in Europe and the New World a scientific language was employed to continue discriminatory treatment of women seeking professional status in medicine. Up to the last decades of the 1800s major teaching centers in the United States participated in efforts to exclude women. Professors of physiology and medicine from Boston and New York interpreted evidence from science to this end. They proclaimed the harm that the entry of women would do not only to the profession but to females. They claimed that women, individually and collectively, were mentally, physically and emotionally unfit for medical education and practice. Chauvinistic descriptions of her "head (as) almost too small for intellect and just enough for love" expressed the tone prevailing among medical leadership in the United States (Morgan 1983). But a mere millennium of uncongeniality did not intimidate some women from seeking entry to medical studies. After twelve attempts at admission Elizabeth Blackwell became the first woman formally accepted in the United States (Longo 1985). Unfortunately her acceptance did not signal a continuing welcome after that initial break-through. While self-selection and determination ultimately produced successful women scholars, practitioners and effective educational and clinical administrators, institutional resistances continued severely to reduce the professional options and resources available to them. This was especially true in the medical schools, hospitals and medical societies of major U.S. eastern cities. For example the Philadelphia County Medical Society supported a resolution to "expel from its ranks any member who consulted with a woman doctor or taught at the all-women's medical college" (Longo 1985). Thus women, driven by necessity, founded colleges for female physicians and surgeons and infirmaries for the care of women and children. *Doctors Wanted — No Women Need Apply* refers particularly to the reception of women M.D.s in the male-dominated east coast medical community (Walsh 1977). In contrast, the openness of western states and territories was more inviting. Young women physicians experienced professional and institutional acceptance as they approached the frontier. The title of a newly published volume captures the pleasure of this turn of events. Its title, *Send Us a Lady Physician,* is derived from correspondence to Dr. Jane Preston, the Dean of Women's College of Pennsylvania. She recounts the frequent requests she received for her graduates to work in communities in the developing west (Abram 1985).

Expansion in numbers of women M.D.s occurred at the turn of the century with the unregulated surge of U.S. proprietary schools. Flexner's influence in the early 1900s contracted those numbers sharply. When competition for places in surviving medical schools became keen, the entrance of women was disproportionately diminished or curtailed. By 1914 women constituted only 4% of all medical students. In the 1930s about 25% of U.S. schools still had total barriers to women. All male programs again opened up to women during World War II, and only one such holdout remained by 1960 (Heins 1985). Before the start of the marked upswing in admission of women in the mid 1960s the fraction of women among total medical students stayed in the 6–7% range. But in the past 20 years entry, enrollment, and graduation data show a climb in numbers of participating women unique in the history of the profession. By 1986–87 about 37% of entering medical students were female.

As doors to and within the profession opened and women entered in significant numbers they have gradually moved across successive frontiers

TABLE 4.1. *Number (and percent) of Women in First-Year Classes U.S. Medical Schools, 1929–30 to 1985–86, Selected Years*

1929–30	219 (4.5)
1939–40	296 (5.0)
1949–50	387 (5.5)
1959–60	494 (6.0)
1969–70	929 (9.0)
1970–71	1228 (11.0)
1874–75	3264 (22.4)
1980–81	4758 (28.7)
1984–85	5469 (33.4)

(Heins 1985)

of professional advancement. An increased rate of admission was the precursor of larger numbers of women in postgraduate residency programs, and, after a time lag, in professional practice and academia.

TABLE 4.2. *Number of Women in Residency Programs (All) Selected Years*

1970	705
1973	953
1976	2132
1983	17566
1985	19562

A 1984 report projects a tripling of women physicians by the year 2000. They would then account for about 20% of the total U.S. physician work force (140,000 out of 700,000). In the following pages we describe features of the career world of contemporary U.S. women in medicine, issues they must address, and suggest how their growing presence may influence the medical profession (Bowman 1986).

PRODUCTIVITY

The "scientific" objections to women in medicine due to their physical disabilities and mental incapacities became outmoded once their performances exposed those premises as false. Arguments for exclusion by gender then shifted to the diseconomies of their low professional productivity. Withdrawal of a woman during medical school (a probability often posed to female applicants by admissions officers) was viewed as the tragic loss of a potential career tract in medicine for the displaced male candidate. Expectations that her interests were merely transient, that she would marry, have children and be unavailable for practice, held great credibility. This hypothesis evoked sharp antagonism toward women. It was necessary for a female candidate whose personal goals included having a family artfully to dodge that issue. Others internalized the projected professional "norm" by accepting celibacy and chose to forego motherhood as an opportunity cost of membership in the profession. This provided a measure of the seriousness of purpose of women aspiring to practice medicine, their willingness to withstand personal sacrifice, and the unconscionable degree of manipulation and coercion to which they were subjected.

The historical record refutes arguments of low productivity at anywhere near predicted levels. But the continuing inflexibilities of medical educators and the disinclination to recognize and support the value and necessity of familial and societal demands on women physicians suggest that the spirit of earlier insensitivity still lingers. Despite multiple demands women are taking and keeping places in all facets of medical careers. Recent reports document continued closing of the relatively minor gap in their productivity compared to male doctors (Bobula 1980; Brooke 1982). Except for specific and usually brief interruptions for childbirth, and despite the disproportionate responsibilities for child-rearing and household management, little differences exist in the hours of work by men and women M.D.s

There are few empiric studies of differences in academic achievement and attributes among male and female students. One such study in the early 1980s followed three classes over a period of six years each in a combined Bachelor of Arts — Doctor of Medicine (B.A.-M.D.) degree

TABLE 4.3. *Active Women Physicians in U.S. Selected Years*

Year	% Active	% Active Full Time
1881	88.0	—
1943	92.0	90.0
1953	87.5	—
1963	91.0	66.0
1969	100.0	60.0
1976	84.0	76.0
1981	92.5	—
Estimate	97.9*	

* Active women physicians under 40 years old
(Heins 1985)

TABLE 4.4. *Hours* Worked Per Week Men and Women Physicians 1978–79*

Speciality	Men	Women
General practice	49.1	53.1
Internal medicine	47.8	46.3
Obstetrics–gynecology	52.8	46.9
Pediatrics	47.8	45.7
Psychiatry	40.5	36.2
Other medical specialties	43.8	40.5
Other surgical specialties	49.0	44.0
All	48.2	45.4

* Hours are self-reported for patient care only (administrative activities are not included)
(Mitchell 1984)

program. It found no statistical differences in percentages of withdrawal and dismissals. Data on performances measured by external test batteries such as National Boards, and by faculty evaluation, show no appreciable quantitative differences among medical students and advanced trainees by gender (Arnold 1981).

Any intent on the part of medical educators to retain students who are admitted to medical school until graduation now results in few pregraduation departures compared with earlier decades. Withdrawal patterns for women have shown a decreasing trend. When withdrawals by women do occur they are more often associated with personal rather than academic reasons (Barondess 1981). Therefore educators concerned with modification of drop-out rates should consider the impact of extra-academic demands.

In advanced training and practice the impact of career interruptions extends beyond the woman herself. They also influence the schedules and

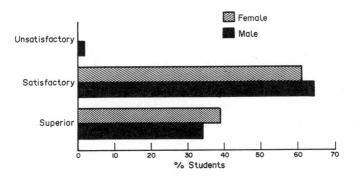

FIG. 2. Mean Level of Clinical Performance By Medical Students in their Elective Year (Arnold 1981)

workloads of her colleagues. The almost inevitable conflicts arising from unattenuated career demands which do not take into account the role of reproduction for women professionals are too obvious to ignore. Yet socially indispensable as those roles may be, supportive response from the medical profession has come more slowly than from business or law. Perhaps this exemplifies a reversion to tenacious former practices of the medical establishment to discourage women from its ranks. Otherwise why should contemporary women physicians in childbearing and childrearing years be subjected to more stringent expectations in respects to reproductive functions than are other employed women? Societal accommodation, i.e., pregnancy leave and return to position, are not beyond the ingenuity and coping capability of those training and employing women physicians. The discriminating assumption that extreme personal sacrifice is the quid pro quo for women in medicine may even now account for footdragging and recalcitrance in coming to reasonable terms with these realities so germane to human life.

As a basis for sex-related comparisons of productivity it is interesting to note that when 120 women with doctoral degrees in mathematics and the sciences were interviewed it was determined that women publish less than men. But marriage and family obligation did not explain the gender difference. Married women with children publish as much as their single female colleagues. Both men and women publish at a lower rate early in their careers regardless of degree of domestic responsibilities (Cole 1987). In academic medicine productivity is similarly often measured by the number of publications a physician authors. Although no comprehensive, quantified study of physician publications by sex and marital status exists inferences about publication experience have been drawn from the known fact that women have not been promoted at the same rate as male faculty in medical schools. No causal associations have established a relationship between these facts.

A primary indicator of productivity in all areas, including medicine, is income earned. The number of hours spent practicing medicine is less correlated to physicians' earnings than are other factors such as specialty. Virtually every study of the subject has shown that women physicians earn less than their male counterparts (Heins 1985; Langwell 1982; Rinke 1981).

Some studies of productivity measure hours worked per week and weeks worked per year. Older surveys disclosed differences of up to 40% fewer hours of lifetime practice by women M.D.s (Lanska 1984). Within the last decade a number of reports show a closing of the gap in work hours analyzed by sex. Occasional reports demonstrate excessive hours worked per week by women M.D.s (Curry 1983).

The evolution of salaried employment and office-based practices by doctors have influenced changes in traditional standards of productivity. Women physicians are disproportionately represented in office-based specialties and salaried work arrangements which allow for set hours (i.e., establishing both minimum and maximum working hours). These formal work schedules also militate against the inclination of self-employed professionals to exaggerate their subjective estimates of hours worked. Barondess reported that, as of the mid-70s, for women physicians whose activities were in patient care, 49% were in office-based and 51% in hospital-based practice (Barondess 1981). Shifts in type of practice organization, especially from solo to group or staff affiliation, also allow for greater planning for a balance in the allocation of time between professional and private agendas. Given these developments it is interesting to note the decreasing disparity in gender-specific work efforts. A sex-related differential in worktime of about 10% is estimated. Married women M.D.s work fewer hours than unmarried M.D.s. A difference is also demonstrated between women M.D.s with preschool children and male M.D.s of the same parental status. While male physicians on salary work fewer hours than independent male M.D.s, a comparable distinction does not apply to women in the two forms of practice (Mitchell 1984).

A longitudinal view of careers of older women physicians has been presented in a follow-up study of women who entered Johns Hopkins Medical School and Case Western Reserve in 1946. Of the entire cohort of 29 women M.D.s followed for 34 years, four-fifths reported full-time work and averaged in excess of 40 hours per week (including about 20% who worked less than full time). Part-time work early in their careers accommodated giving birth and child rearing. The 69% who were mothers produced an average of 3.2 children per family. Thirty-five years after entering medical school these women want to continue medical practice and few are anticipating retirement in the immediate future. All but one said they would "do it again" and recommended a medical career to other women (Lerner 1981). These results are consistent with other surveys in which working women physicians express high career satisfaction. In one such study of women physicians, 60% recommend medical careers to others compared with 50% of men (Bowman 1986).

Traditionally the scarcity of places in medical schools and the shortage of physicians in the United States made less than full productive status by women physicians a source of severe criticism. Those conditions are now significantly altered (Lanska 1984). A dropping ratio of applicants to acceptances in medical schools and an excess of physicians in practice should increase tolerance for women in medicine to deal with reproductive and professional roles without playing superwoman. Changes in patterns of practice organizations, recommendations by specialty and American Medical Association spokespersons, and a developing body of legislative actions and judicial opinions governing personnel norms and job rights related to pregnancy will undoubtedly assist. The growing number of women within the field of medicine will, per se, have an effect on promoting transitions to policies which recognize and support the multiple human responsibilities of its members.

SPECIALIZATION AND PRACTICE

A host of factors determine specialty choice by physicians. The choice is influenced by internal motivation, cultural, esthetic and parental influences, mentor example, and financial and other practical incentives. For women, overt and de facto exclusion has constituted an effective disincentive for advanced training and practice, particularly in the surgical specialties. We are just approaching a time of conspicuous changes from past patterns. The widened aspirations of greater numbers of young women are now, for the first time in history, matched by opportunities in an expanded inventory of specialty options available to them.

Schermerhorn et al. surveyed women physicians in practice on factors that contributed to their specialty choices. In this study intellectual challenge was the primary reason given for deciding on a specialty. This was followed by preferences for the skills used and the kinds of patients associated with the specialty choice. Pragmatic considerations such as training time, prestige and income were placed low on the scale of criteria (Schermerhorn et al. 1986).

These findings are compatible with traditional observations on sex-stereotyped specialty selection. U.S.-trained women M.D.s have disproportionately elected to practice in five areas: Primary or General Medicine, Pediatrics, Physical Medicine, Psychiatry and Preventive Medicine. The surgical specialties, found persistently less welcoming, were accessible most commonly through gynecology (Harris, 1981; Weisman, 1980). Clearly income has been an elastic incentive in these choices.

The federally commissioned report on Graduate Medicine Education (GMENAC) forecasts a surplus of physicians by 1990 for most specialties. The specialty choices of women, noted above, tend to cluster in areas where shortages or the absence of an excess of doctors have been predicted. Thus although the diffusion into specialty patterns for men and women are becoming more similar, distribution of more women into their traditional specialty choices would tend to alleviate shortages rather than exaggerate surpluses (AMA 1985).

Data on women in residency programs in 1984 show that they are now dispersed in training programs to prepare for practice in all medical specialties. The only subspecialty with no women in training was vascular surgery. In fact the percentage of residents who were women increased from 19 in 1978 to 26 in 1985. In 1977 over one-third of the specialties had no women residents; by 1985 women were in all the major specialties (See Table 4.5). Nonetheless, high percentages of women residents (greater than 30% of trainees) still choose to practice in "conventional" fields.

TABLE 4.5. *Number (and percent) Women Residents by Specialty, September 1984*

	Number	Percent
Allergy and Immunology	67	25.9
Anesthesiology	750	19.2
Colon and Rectal Surgery	3	7.3
Dermatology	294	37.7
Dermatopathology	5	21.7
Emergency Medicine	225	20.3
Family Practice	1789	24.1
Internal Medicine	4432	24.3
Neurological Surgery	40	5.7
Neurology	343	24.3
Nuclear Medicine	55	27.0
Obstetrics-Gynecology	1784	38.6
Ophthalmology	281	17.9
Orthopedic Surgery	99	3.4
Otolaryngology	120	11.4
Pathology	858	34.8
Blood banking	11	32.3
Forensic pathology	10	28.5
Neuropathology	8	18.1
Pediatrics	2859	47.4
Pediatric cardiology	30	21.7
Neonatal-perinatal medicine	82	37.9
Physical Medicine and Rehabilitation	214	30.0
Plastic Surgery	57	13.2
Preventive Medicine		
General	60	33.1
Aerospace medicine	5	4.2
Occupational medicine	25	28.7
Public health	10	40.0
Combined general		
preventive/public health	18	31.0
Psychiatry	1678	36.8
Child psychiatry	260	50.0
Radiology, diagnostic	686	21.5
Radiology, diagnostic (nuclear)	25	28.4
Radiology, therapeutic	125	24.0
Surgery	909	11.1
Pediatric surgery	6	22.2
Vascular surgery	0	0.0
Thoracic surgery	17	3.8
Urology	40	21.9
Transitional 1-year program	317	21.4
Total	18,603	24.9

(Bowman 1986)

About 39% of women residents train in internal medicine or pediatrics. Another 30% are training in obstetrics/gynecology, psychiatry and family medicine. As the increased proportion of female medical students graduate into specialty training it is anticipated that doors that traditionally permitted only limited entry will be further challenged. But countervailing influences, such as fewer residency positions available, may spark a return to discriminatory practices especially in specialties faced with excess numbers of applicants. Therefore specialties with relative under-representation of women will continue to warrant monitoring in future years.

Training programs often have not been as responsive as desired to the multiple roles of women in medicine. Part of this stems from the view of training as an initiation rite which must be endured prior to passage into specialty status. For some medical educators repetition of their own postgraduate training experiences remains the dominant model of refer-ence. Such attitudes can be deeply embedded and so distorted that they are perceived as virtues by their perpetrators. Fortunately the influence of more progressive forces has been felt recently and they are gradually being substituted for the less rational tactics. Meanwhile women physicians are influencing mentors and colleagues in local settings, individually and through professional organizations which address the politics of program revision. The collective efforts of women continue to be effective in the evolutionary process through which women have progressed in seeking full admission to the medical profession. Women physicians are still working to define terms of their roles in the profession which are compatible with their total obligations.*

Several recent studies reflect the status and experiences of women in particular specialties. Characteristics common among women specialists include higher parental socioeconomic and educational status (Goldstein 1981; McNamara 1985). Distinctive characteristics and attitudes define women planning to enter surgery. Their family of origin tended to be upper strata, and they were more likely to have physician fathers, and mothers with college educations. As a group they were more similar to male classmates in placing value on high professional income. Women medical students oriented toward surgery expected to make significant sacrifices in other areas of their lives to attain their professional goals. For example, they accepted the idea of an 80-hour or longer work week during training. They were closer in attitudes reflecting competitiveness, dominance and independence to male students than to other women medical students. Although they had less than average accessibility to or encouragement from role models they often had strong family support (Burnley 1986;

* AMA Ad Hoc Committee on Women Physicians (1984) advised that a written policy on maternity leave for women residents be developed which provides for meeting educational requirements, for patient care and for treatment of the pregnant resident and her colleagues.

Kinder 1985). Urology, one of the least female populated specialties, had only 22 board certified women specialists in the United States in January 1985 yet, like their sisters in surgery and other specialties, these pioneers reported career satisfaction (Gillespie 1985). A sidelight to the historical review of 29 female urologists noted that each and every one was either an only child or the eldest among her siblings.

Efforts to test for professional support among specialty colleagues by gender reveal that biases, including less inclination to refer patients to women practitioners, were evidenced. This pattern decreased as professional contacts increased; however, a negative experience with a woman M.D. tended to provoke persisting adverse sex-stereotyping by male M.D.s (Martin 1986). In view of these remnants of discriminatory behavior it is somewhat remarkable that women respondents typically report higher professional satisfaction than do their male counterparts and they enthusiastically recommend that young women enter the specialty they have chosen.

The hurdles of undergraduate medical education and residency so fully engage some candidates that they ignore or defer attention to quality of life questions relating to the period beyond training. Matching the preferences of the individual doctor to opportunities within a sphere of practice requires a careful and personalized exploration of both the person and the position. Tallying the advantages and disadvantages of post-training lifestyle ought to occur BEFORE the young professional stumbles into a trial-and-error approach to practice decisions. Women physicians are learning to be more specific in their inquiries about potential positions. Planning ahead avoids damaging experiences. Careful career explorations are important complements to the advice of mentors and to other informal influences on the young woman physician.

The women's movement can be credited for enhancing self-esteem. This generation of women physicians is less likely than their predecessors to be coerced into patterns imitative of male professionals. Competency is no longer viewed as a predominantly male trait. Dr. Estelle Ramey has championed the *vive la difference* notion which faces up to the realities of disparities between males and females from biological and social perspectives. She exhorts women to acknowledge rather than to deny such differences. The traditional sense of inferiority trained into women has largely been replaced by self-assessments of parity in women's abilities relative to their brothers'. Increasingly it is recognized that the combination of complementing strengths of male and female approaches to professional tasks can produce an enriched result not otherwise attainable. But at the same time women must try to be scrupulously honest about facing the opportunity costs and the trade-offs between personal and professional spheres. This may lead to selection of a specialty area compatible with her non-professional life-pattern projections. It also requires making explicit choices and seeking professional activities that encompass preferred tasks and contact with the kind of patients she enjoys serving.

Societal and organizational changes are aiding in mainstreaming and streamlining women M.D.s' professional careers. The "oddity" image of the isolated woman practitioner has virtually disappeared as a stereotype. In some regards public acceptance of women doctors has proceeded more quickly than has professional assimilation. For example, it is frequently the expressed pressure of patients that triggers male gynecologists to bring a female specialist into their partnership. The swing away from private practice, solo or group, toward salaried positions has, as mentioned earlier, opened up contractual arrangements for part- and full-time work options which are attractive to women. The advantage of "sovereign control of his practice" so highly prized by many male independent practitioners has had less appeal for female M.Ds. With salaried status and institutional affiliation the M.D.-employee gains predictability of the work schedule while being able to delegate the often-difficult task of planning clinical coverage to administrative personnel within the organization.

Reasonable estimates of the time which can be allocated to professional activities need to be derived from close consideration of total commitments. Women M.D.s and those working with them are recognizing that certain phases of their career require modification from traditional work patterns instituted for and by males. With planning, women can objectively outline competing interests and, in advance, allocate time realistically. Not to do this only temporarily represses realities which inevitably emerge. Unrealistic agreements to do the unaccomplishable generate failure in meeting obligations. Precaution and foresight can avoid having to face the adverse results of serious overcommitment: disgruntled associates, personal anxiety, exhaustion, decremental performance, and even compromised professional standing.

WOMEN IN MEDICAL EDUCATION

Women physicians had limited access to faculty positions until recent decades. Available positions in medical education were at the "invisible" level, i.e., unrecorded in printed materials, or in terminal tracts such as Research Associate. Upward mobility through the professional ranks was for practical purposes confined to women in all-female institutions. Yet the presence of women as medical researchers and educators had great impact on the professional development of generations of (mostly male) physicians. Dr. Eleanor Shore cites that one such example, Dr. Louise Eisenhardt at Harvard from 1923–33, did research in neuropathology and taught at the post-graduate level. References to her presence or her contributions are not hinted at in the faculty records. In spite of that "oversight," a colleague estimated in 1959 that Dr. Eisenhardt had helped train over 70% of the more than 700 M.D.s who had taken board examinations in neurosurgery (Shore 1984).

Acknowledgment of the contributions of women through academic promotion has also come slowly. A 1981 study of promotion patterns in all clinical departments of a prominent U.S. medical school revealed marked differences by gender in the years of service before advancement in faculty rank (Wallis 1981).

TABLE 4.6. *Combined Data From All Clinical Departments of a Northeastern Medical College*

	Total No.	No. of Years of Service Before Promotion	
		Median (Range)	Mean (SD)
Professor			
M	95	12.8(0–32)	12.3(8.6)
F	5	21.0(15–26)*	20.8(5.3)*
Clinical Professor			
M	47	18.1(0–29)	16.4(8.1)
F	3	31.0(15–26)*	27.7(8.5)
Associate Professor			
M	78	7.5(0–35)	8.3(6.7)
F	12	7.5(1–31)	10.3(9.6)
Clinical Associate Professor			
M	187	10.7(0–31)	10.1(7.4)
F	31	11.5(0–24)	11.0(8.3)
Assistant Professor			
M	186	2.8(0–23)	3.4(3.9)
F	31	3.0(0–16)	3.3(3.4)
Clinical Assistant Professor			
M	356	4.5(0–34)	5.9(6.2)
F	47	8.6(0–32)	8.7(7.6)
Total			
M	949	—	—
F	112	—	—

* p .02 by Student's test; p .03 by Wilcoxon's rank sum test.
 p .008 by Student's test; p .02 by Wilcoxon's rank sum test.
 p .005 for single, combined contrast comparing men and women within academic ranks. Square roots were applied to data to help satisfy normality and equal variance requirements of analysis of variance (Wallis 1981).

In spite of their invisibility and inadequate rewards the proportions of women on medical faculties to all women physicians was greater than the comparable ratio for their male colleagues.

A small increase in full-time women M.D.s and/or Ph.D. faculty members (from about 13% to 17%) occurred in the 20-year period before the mid-1980s (Shore 1984). While this is a relatively favorable representation of women in academia compared to the overall proportion of women in medicine their distribution has been consistently sparse at higher ranks (5% of professors) and concentrated at "entry" levels. Even in academic pediatrics where women have an established presence, the lag in advancement remains (See Table 4.7).

Basic science disciplines and clinical faculties have shown some increase in the percentage of women faculty in this decade but of course this does not yet reflect the dramatic increase of women entrants into the profession in the same period. Medical academia will soon begin to register the impact. As the augmented population wave is distributed over the professional ranks and across administrative assignments a boost in the presence of women faculty, including placement in advanced ranks and administrative positions, should occur. At present only about 2% of department chairs are women, and a significant proportion of these hold acting or interim status. Although only two women served as deans of American medical schools in the decade 1975–85 the number of women assistant deans rose from 11.7% to 18.7%. A three-fold increase in associate deans (3.3% to 9.9%) took place in the same period. Unfortunately these positions, primarily concerned with student and curricular affairs, are seldom the route to top leadership appointments in medical education (Braslow 1981).

TABLE 4.7. *Distribution of Faculty in All Departments of Pediatrics**

Rank	Male		Female		% of Rank (M/F)
	No	%	No	%	
Professor	880	23.9	134	9.5	86.8/13.2
Associate Professor	863	23.4	275	19.5	75.8/24.2
Assistant Professor	1,444	39.2	640	45.4	69.3/30.7
Instructor	434	11.8	312	22.1	58.2/41.8
Other	35	0.9	43	3.0	44.9/55.1
Unknown	31	0.8	7	0.5	81.6/18.4
Total	3,687	100.0	1,411	100.0	
% of Total	72.3		27.7		

* From Turner, K.: Women in Medicine Statistics. Washington, D.C., Association of American Medical Colleges, 1982 (Morgan et al. 1983).

TABLE 4.8. *Distribution of Medical School Administrative Positions 1975–76 and 1982–83**

| | 1975–76 | | 1982–83 | |
	Men	Women	Men	Women
Dean	119	0	126	1
Associate Dean	369	13 (3.4%)	536	56 (9.5%)
Assistant Dean	220	29 (11.7%)	279	61 (17.9%

* From K. Turner, personal communication, Washington, D.C., Association of American Medical Colleges, September 1982 (Morgan et al. 1983).

A 1983 Supplement to *Pediatrics* focused on women in various sectors of that field. One paper, "Women in Pediatric Academia", pointed out major "issues of concern to women physicians in medical academia." They can be summarized as:

1. Personal and professional role conflict, especially regarding time for reproductive functions.
2. Low proportionate representation on medical faculties by sex.
3. Changes in women's specialty choice options resulting in a smaller pool of potential female faculty in traditionally women's areas.
4. Slow and limited advancements.
5. Adverse effects of geographic factors and relative immobility.
6. Salary discrimination (Morgan et al. 1983).

Obviously while there is cause for optimism in recent developments and projections the agenda has not cleared in the years since this compilation was printed.

MARRIAGE, PREGNANCY AND PARENTING

Women physicians now marry in the same proportion as women generally. But trends indicate that they marry a number of years later and have fewer children than the average American female (Battle 1983). Women physicians are comparable to women in other scholarly professions in terms of their marital patterns, pregnancy and parenting experience, but different in that more than half of married female physicians are married to physicians (Myers 1984).

There has been a great deal of discussion in the last decade about role conflict for female physicians and the development of policies to accommodate pregnancy during residency, leaves for parenting, part-time employment and flexible work schedules. In addition there have been a few longitudinal (Ducker 1986; Lerner 1981) studies to analyze the effects of marriage, pregnancy, and motherhood on female physicians.

A compilation of the numerous editorial and experimental papers reviewed (Tuohey 1985; Eisenberg 1981; Angell 1982; Myers 1984; Brown 1982, 1986) indicates that flexibility on the part of residency directors, house officers, colleagues and husbands is the most important ingredient in the successful resolution of conflict arising from the competing demands of career and motherhood. Female physicians who become mothers usually have at least one pregnancy during their residency training. If some adjustments are made in their schedule during the late stages of pregnancy and a 2–3 month leave is possible following the birth, most female physicians report satisfaction with their dual roles (Baucom-Copeland 1983; Porter 1983). Unfortunately, many institutions are unprepared for pregnancy in the house staff. In a study of 63 of the Harvard-affiliated residency programs four-fifths of the programs had no maternity leave policy. Practicing physicians often state that their choice of a specialty, practice-setting, and desire for administration and/or academic responsibilities are influenced by their desire to spend time with their families. In addition these women usually report that they eliminated discretionary practices such as participation in sports, organizations, and professional societies rather than significantly cut back on professional work hours or valued time with their families. As a result the average number of hours spent in medical practice are only slightly lower for female physicians with families than those of their male counterparts (Sayres 1986).

Research data about marriage and family and the practice of women physicians confirm our intuition that women have legitimate concerns about being successful and satisfied in their roles. Women physicians, in a number of studies, have greater disparity between their expectations and their experiences when they are compared with male physicians regarding pregnancy, parenting and family life. Female medical students and residents expect to share child care, household chores and financial responsibilities equally with their husbands. Their male peers expect to participate much less in child care and household chores and to contribute more financially (Bonar 1982). Obviously since many of these young physicians will marry one another some of these expectations will be disappointed. A study in which male and female residents and faculty were surveyed about their attitudes toward parenthood during residency training indicated that all respondents thought it was more difficult for the women residents to become a parent during residency. Similarly respondents felt that their departments had a more favorable attitude toward the resident with a pregnant spouse then toward the pregnant resident herself. (Shapiro 1982).

Some researchers have compared and analyzed ways of managing the combined responsibilities of motherhood and residency training. Specific recommendations have been made about timing of the pregnancy (first, second, third year), scheduling vacation and conference time, negotiating with the father for shared responsibilities, choosing day care and obtaining support within the program. Consideration of managing dual-doctor families have also been discussed. Doctors Esther and David Nash have produced a "Dual Doctor Families" newsletter as one source of support and information sharing (Brooke 1982).

Policy implications regarding pregnancy and child care needs of employees, for all sectors of the health care system, have been suggested by numerous writers. First of all policies must reflect the needs of the setting and the practitioners. These policies should include part-time residencies and employment, leave of absence and some flexibility in work hours.

STRESS AND SOCIAL SUPPORT

Sex discrimination and role stress have been reported by female physicians for decades. In the early 1970s studies of stress among female medical students and residents reported that female physicians developed different behaviors and attitudes than their male counterparts. When they did assimilate into their defined roles it was often painful (Poirier 1986; Barondess 1981). Additional studies report higher levels of anxiety and feelings of isolation among female medical students and residents than in their male peers. Young female physicians have attributed these feelings to problems with balancing their personal and professional roles (Elliot 1986). A longitudinal study of women physicians at two points in their careers focused on levels of stress, and the extent and nature of career interruptions. When the telephone survey was first conducted during 1971–72 there were 93 respondents with a mean age of 50.8 years (56% of the sample under age 50). Of these 55% were married and 50% were mothers with a mean of 2.6 children. Twenty-six percent of the children were less than 7 years old. Ten years later, although there were some dropouts, the women were again asked about role strain, career interruptions and personal characteristics. At both times the female physicians reported an average 45.7-hour work week. At the time of the first interview 59% of the female physicians felt their personal lives suffered because of their professional roles. The components of their personal lives that were most affected were: personal well-being (49%), children (29%) and marriage (24%). At the second interview only 35% indicated that their personal life suffered at least moderately. This time social life was the most affected area. The physicians reported having no time for social activities, friends, hobbies, travel or other leisure pursuits. Overall this study showed some decrease in stress with age, with levels of perceived strain not related to number of children or to involvement in or importance of family life. There was, as expected, a negative relationship between the level of the husband's supportiveness and the woman's feeling that her personal life suffered (Ducker 1986). This is consistent with the belief that social support is an essential ingredient in the maintenance of highly demanding roles.

Social support groups, sponsorships, mentor-relationships, and women's programs have become more accessible in the last 15 years (Hammond 1981; Lorber 1981, 1986; Sirridge 1985). These new groups and programs complement the long-standing and traditional support systems of family, and friendship among classmates and/or colleagues. Women physicians need other women physicians as colleagues, role models, mentors, sponsors, and friends (Battle 1981). The camaraderie of increased numbers of female physicians may provide a spontaneous framework or induce more formal programs for increased social support. These activities typically offer assistance with information exchange about clinical, administrative and other professional matters as well as their relation to personal interests of women in medicine.

A first and second year elective course in "Parenting and Professionalism" has been offered at the New Jersey Medical School (Brodkin 1982) to address the needs, problems and resolutions necessary to maintain both a successful career in medicine and a satisfying experience with parenting. The courses look at both perspectives — the child's best interests and the parent's well-being — in order to help students analyze their future choices. This approach of anticipating and dealing with stress is reportedly well received by the students. It is an important way to predict and modify stress.

Female physicians have long been exposed to sexist language in medical publications. In a survey of members of the American Medical Women's Association women under the age of 30 express the greatest objection to sex-role stereotyping and generic use of masculine word forms. (Cox 1981). Now that the number of women admitted to medical school has grown to over 35% women are voicing their objections and making suggestions for change. This process will evolve at a slow rate unless women physicians express their strong objections to both publishers and authors.

The dual discrimination experienced by black female physicians has been noted but only recently studied. Most of us are aware of the efforts to increase enrollment of minority medical students since the 1960s. However, black women currently represent only 10% of all black physicians. This percentage will significantly increase during this decade since 44% of black medical students are now female. (Adams 1986; Blout 1984). A recent study looked at career satisfaction and conflict in this group. Although the study sample size was small (N=39) nearly 90% of the women were satisfied with their careers and 69% reported minimal or infrequent role conflict (Lovelace 1985). Although the black female physician faces both sexism and racism, Janice C. Lovelace speculates that these minority women come equipped with strong support systems and many internal strengths. Their culture expects women to work and the individual women studied coped with stress with expectations and behaviors that were aggressive and forthright. Unlike their white contemporaries the mothers of black women M.D.s usually worked outside the home during the 1950s and 1960s. The daughters are often beneficiaries of both verbal encouragement and direct examples from their primary role models. The women studied expected to change and adapt to their multiple role and to have positive influences on others to do the same.

WOMEN'S HEALTH ISSUES

Women's health has been defined as all health issues that have a female component. Conditions or diseases included in most discussions are those related to the x chromosome, to the female reproductive system, physiologic responses (including metabolism) and psychosocial responses. During the first half of the twentieth century research on women's health focused primarily on obstetrics and gynecology. Today there is a much broader view with both research and practice expanding their scope. These changes have dramatically influenced some female physicians (Marieskind 1984). In the past, when men set the agendas in search of scientific and medical truths, masculine bias was pervasive. Women scientists and physicians are now asking additional and somewhat different questions and making observations from a female perspective. Undoubtedly this important addition to the research and clincial sphere will lead to new scientific knowledge with special application to womens' health.

Occupational Medicine is one field that makes clear the importance of looking at sex differences in the context of disease causation. Toxic exposure levels, stress responses, injuries, and acute illness at the work sites are significantly different for the sexes. Research in Occupational Medicine, and more generally the practice experiences of all physicians treating members of the workforce (now 42% female), are evolving in light of new information. Studies of occupational illness, accidents and long-term consequences of work-site exposures are now universally done taking the variable of sex into account. Clinical practices of internal medicine, family medicine and general medicine have not always kept pace with research finding in women's health, and to some degree research has been inadequate in treating sex as a significant care-related variable. For example, diseases which are of major clinical significance among males have been extensively studied, while specific characteristics and manifestations of diseases which have unique impact on females have been less emphasized. Recent research in disease susceptibility, the pathologic course and responses to therapy are beginning to address the sex-specific courses of certain diseases. For example, employment, per se, has been found not to be a Coronary Heart Disease (CHD) risk factor for women. Single working women, in one study, had the lowest rates of CHD (Haynes 1984) when compared with married working women and men. However, more research is needed to look at geographic, occupational and other stress- and disease-inducing conditions for women. Drug therapy is perhaps the most-used treatment in medicine. Women use more prescription drugs than men and they experience more adverse side effects (controlling for number of drugs and dose). An increasing body of research suggests that women have different metabolic and physiological responses to drugs as they move through the life cycle (Hamilton 1983). The significance of these responses in women is beginning to be examined in drug trials which distinguish between the effects on patients according to sex. New implications and needed suggestions for clinical practice which differentiate health and disease responses by sex are anticipated from this work.

Mental health issues of women are important in the practice of psychiatry and, indeed, in all of medical practice. Women physicians are in a position to recognize these issues, study them, and treat them from a knowledge- and sensitivity-perspective not accorded by many traditional psychotherapists (Miller 1984). In addition to the treatment of patients, the female physician needs to have an awareness of stresses and mental health problems experienced by her peers and by herself. As the female physician's role evolves, the nature of stressors encountered change. Finding appropriate ways to cope with them is a dynamic and continuing challenge. It is important to have more awareness of the role of the female physician as provider and participant in prevention and therapeutic measures. Such work can have a positive impact on the level of mental health in our society.

The aging process is an increasingly important area in women's health. Longevity is a function of interacting and interdependent genetic, biological, environmental and social factors (Ory 1984). The movement of women into the labor force, the change in women's health and social habits and the influences of the practice of modern medicine may all alter the way we age and our longevity. Specific concerns of women's health and aging, such as osteoporosis, have been largely ignored even though they consititute major causes of disability and high medical-care costs. We have only begun to provide the research and clinical attention such entities deserve. Women doctors can serve as advocates for this work as well as playing more direct roles as investigators and clinicians.

As women become physicians in increasing numbers their collective influence has and will continue to be felt. Women physicians will undoubtedly have effects on all aspects of the professional role, ranging from the doctor-patient relationship, the doctor-to-doctor relationship, the doctor-family relationship and the doctor in society. Evidence suggests that women in medicine are humanistically motivated, aware of the environmental as well as biological influences, and inclined to emphasize public and patient education in approaching health and illness (Brown 1982; Hayes 1981; McGoldrick 1983). The female physician brings with her characteristics such as intuitive skills learned in her own experiences, as well as scientific knowledge to give fuller dimensions to her practice of medicine.

No scientist denies the influence of interviewer or observer bias. Collectively male scientists, using their masculine perspective, have influenced the questions they asked and the knowledge base we accept. A comparable process by female scientists will amplify the scope and context of future scientific inquiry. As women medical scientists and female physicians ask more questions about physiological functioning, biological processes, environmental and genetic influence, and psychosocial factors the systemic influence of women may, for the first time, emerge as a source of their special contributions. Simultaneously, in concrete ways, women are likely to bring about changes in the ways medicine is practiced; in workload and time patterns, in the way they socialize, in their responses to hierarchical and other organizational structures, and in the way they relate to patients, families and society. It is our privilege to observe and evaluate these changes and it is our responsibility to guide their directions.

CONCLUSIONS

During our lifetimes women have become a significant and sizeable force in many specialties of medicine. We have moved from outside the mainstream of medicine to become insiders in many settings. But it is important that we maintain a perspective on where we have been as we move into the ranks and hierarchies of the medical establishment. Women have experienced relative acceptance in medicine before, most recently at the turn of the twentieth century, but there have been ups and downs to these trends. Women have often been accepted without a real acknowledgment of their value and their gender role differences. If they are merely admitted to medicine because external factors facilitate the entry process, women's role will continue to be reactive (Brown 1986). That pattern perpetuates medicine as a man-dominated decision-making system.

Women physicians have the opportunity to expand their roles and to redefine the scope of their involvement with patients and families, other physicians, health care colleagues, and with the businessmen who administer health care. For both men and women physicians, working in an industry that has experienced a sharp rise in the influence of corporate management, the remainder of this century will be a time to protect their professional prerogatives and to influence developing professional priorities. Women physicians can negotiate for parity and full acceptance as part of this process. As women physicians accept shared professional activity and status in the contemporary health care delivery system they will be wise to have eyes wide open to the past, the present and the future.

REFERENCES

Abram, R. J. 1985. Send Us a Lady Physician: Women Doctors in America, 1835–1920. W. W. Norton and Company.

Adams, E. K., and Bazzoli, G. J. 1986. Career plans of women and minority physicians: Implications for health manpower policy. *JAMWA* **41**(1): 17–20.

American Medical Association. 1985–1986. Directory of residency training programs. AMA Publication No. OP-167/5. Chicago, Illinois 1985, Table 10, p. 90.

American Medical Association, 1985–1986. Directory of residency training programs. AMA Publication No. OP-167/5. Chicago, Illinois 1985, Table 10, p. 90.

Angell, M. 1982. Juggling the personal and professional life. *JAMWA* **37**(3): 64–68.

Arnold, L., Willoughby, T. L., Calkins, V., and Jensen, T. 1981. The achievement of men and women in medical school. *JAMWA* **36**(7): 213–221.

Barondess, J. A. 1981. Are women different: Some trends in the assimilation of women in medicine. *JAMWA* **36**(3): 95–104.

Battle, C. U. 1981. The iatrogenic disease called burnout. *JAMWA* **36**(12): 357–359.

Battle, C. U. 1983. Working and motherhood: a view of today's realities. *JAMWA* **38**(4): 103–105.

Baucom-Copeland, S., Copeland, E. T., and Perry, L. L. 1983. The pregnant resident: career conflict? *JAMWA* **38**(4): 103–105.

Blout, M. 1984. Surpassing obstacles: black women in medicine. *JAMWA* **39**(6): 192–195.

Bobula, J. D. 1980. Work patterns, practice characteristics, and income for male and female physicians. *J. of Med. Educ.* **55**: 826–833.

Bonar, J. W., Watson, J. A., and Koester, L. S. 1982. Sex differences in career and family plans of medical students. *JAMWA* **37**(11): 300–303.

Bowman, M., and Gross, M. L. 1986. Overview of research on women in medicine — issue for public policymakers. Public Health Reports **101**(5): 513–521.

Braslow, J. B. 1981. Women in medical education. *NEJ* **304**(19): 1129–1135.

Brodkin, A. M., Shrier, D. K., and Buxton, M. 1982. Parenting and professionalism — a medical school elective. *JAMWA* **37**(9): 227–230.

Brooke, K. L. 1982. Success — an historical perspective. *JAMWA* **37**(12): 330–331.

Brooke, K. L. 1982. Drs. Carol and Ted Nadelson on dual-career marriage. *JAMWA* **37**(11): 292–299.

Brown, S. L., and Klein, R. H. 1982. Woman-power in the medical hierarchy. *JAMWA* **37**(6): 155–164.

Brown, S. L., and Klein, R. H. 1986. Women physicians: casualties of organizational stress. *JAMWA* **41**(3): 79–81.

Burnley, C. S. 1986. Specialization: are women in surgery different? *JAMWA* **41**(5): 144–149.

Cole, J. R., and Zuckerman, H. 1987. Marriage, motherhood and research performance in science. *Scientific American* **256**(2): 119–125.

Cox, B. G., and Lewis, L. A. 1981. Responses of medical women to a survey on sexist language in medical publications. *JAMWA* **36**(1): 15–18.

Curry, L. 1983. The effect of sex on physicians work patterns. *Research in Medicine* Ed., 144.

Ducker, D. G. 1986. Role conflict in women physicians: a longitudinal study. *JAMWA* **41**(1): 14–16.

Eisenberg, L. 1981. The distaff of aesculapius — the married woman as physician. *JAMWA* **36**(2).

Elliot, D. L., and Girard, D. E. 1986. Gender and the emotional impact of internship. *JAMWA* **41**(2): 54–56.

Gillespie, L., Cosgrove, M., Fourcroy, J., and Calmes, S. 1985. Women in Urology: A splash in the pan. *Urology* **XXV**(1): 93–97.

Goldstein, M. Z. 1981. Psychiatrists' life and work patterns: A statewide comparison of women and men. *Am. J. Psych.* **138**:7: 919–924.

Hamilton, J., and Parry, B. 1983. Sex-related differences in clinical drug response: implications for women's health. *JAMWA* **38**(5): 126–132.

Hammond, J. M. 1981. Social support groups, women's programs, and research on gender differences: The bad press for women in medical education literature. *JAMWA* **36**(5): 162–165.

Harris, M. B., and Conley-Muth, M. A. 1981. Sex role stereotypes and medical specialty choice. *JAMWA* **36**(8): 245–252.

Hayes, M. D. 1981. The impact of women physicians on social change in medicine: the evolution of humane health care delivery system. *JAMWA* **36**(2): 82–84.

Haynes, S. G. 1984. Women and coronary heart disease. *JAMWA* **39**(3): 102–105.

Heins, M. 1985. Update: women in medicine. *JAMWA* **40**(2): 43–50.

Introduction. 1983. *Women in Pediatrics.* Pediatric Supplement, 679.

Kinder, B. K. 1985. Women and men as surgeons: are the problems really different? *Current Surgery,* 100–104.

Langwell, K. M. 1982. Differences by sex in economic returns associated with physician specialization. *J. of Health Policies, Policy and Law,* **6**(4): 752–761.

Lanska, M. J., Lanska, D. J., and Rimm, A. A. 1984. Effect of rising percentage of female physicians on projections of physician supply. *J. Med. Educ.,* **59**: 849–855.

Lerner, M. R. 1981. The women: who, where, when and why? *JAMWA* **36**(11): 329–338.

Longo, M. F. 1985. History of women surgeons. *Current Surgery,* 91–93.

Lorber, J. 1981. The limits of sponsorship for women physicians. *JAMWA* **36**(11): 329–338.

Lorber, J. 1986. Sisterhood is synergistic. *JAMWA* **41**(4): 116–119.

Lovelace, J. C. 1985. Career satisfaction and role harmony in Afro-American women physicians. *JAMWA* **40**(4): 108–110.

Marieskind, H. I. 1984. Research in women's health: problems and prospects. *JAMWA* **39**(3): 91–105.

Martin, C. A. 1986. Attitudes towards women in radiology. *JAMWA* **41**(2): 50–53.

McGoldrick, K. E. 1981. The editor's page. *JAMWA* **36**(12): 356.

McGoldrick, K. E. 1983. Humane approaches in the doctor-patient relationship. *JAMWA* **38**(5): 133–135.

McNamara, M. F. 1985. Women surgeons: How much of an impact? *Current Surgery,* 94–99.

Miller, J. B. 1984. Women and mental health. *JAMWA* **39**(3): 97–111.

Mitchell, J. B. 1984. Why do women physician's work fewer hours than men physicians? *Inquiry* **21**: 361–368.

Morgan, B. C., Aplin, E. R., Garrison, L., Hilman, B. C., Howell, D. A., Navarro, A., O'Hare, D., Pittelli, A., Skansi, V., and Tanner, N. M. 1983. Report of the task force on opportunities for women in pediatrics. Pediatric Supplement, **71**(4): 679–714.

Myers, M. F. 1984. Overview: the female physician and her marriage. *Am J. Psych.* **141**(11): 1386–1391.

Ory, M. G. 1984. Women and aging. *JAMWA* **39**(3): 99–101.

Poirier, S. 1986. Role stress in medical education: a literary perspective. *JAMWA* **41**(3): 82–86.

Porter, R. L. 1983. Resident, women, wife, mother: issues for women in training. *JAMWA* **38**(4): 98–102.

Rinke, C. 1981. The economic and academic status of women physicians. *JAMWA* **245**(22): 2305–2306.

Sayres, M., Wyshak, G., Denterlein, G., Apfel, R., Shore, E., and Federman, D. 1986. Pregnancy during residency. *NEJM* **314**(7): 418–423.

Schermerhorn, G. R., Colliver, J. A., Verhulst, S. J., and Schmidt, E. L. 1986. Factors that influence career patterns of women physicians. *JAMWA* **41**(3): 74–78.

Shapiro, J. 1982. Pregnancy during residency: attitudes and policies. *JAMWA* **37**(4): 96–103.

Shore, E. G. 1984. Academia. *JAMWA* **39**(3): 81–83.

Sirridge, M. S. 1985. The mentor system in medicine — how it works for women. *JAMWA* **40**(2): 51–53.

Tuohey, M. K. 1985. Working women, working lovers: the effect of our multiple roles on intimacy. *JAMWA* **40**(3): 92–94.
Wallis, L. A. 1981. Advancement of men and women in medical academia. *JAMWA* **246**(20): 2350–2853.
Walsh, M. R. 1977. *Doctors Wanted: No Women Need Apply: Sexual Barriers in the Medical Profession.* Yale University Press.
Weisman, C. S., Levine, D. M., Steinwachs, D. M., and Chase, G. A. 1980. Male and female physician career patterns: specialty choices and graduate training. *J. Med. Educ.* **55**: 813–825.

3
Impact on Theory and Practice: Resistances to Feminism

Chapter 5

Science and the Construction of Meanings in the Neurosciences*

Ruth Bleier

In a burst of pride about science, its practitioners, and its leading journal, *Science*, Daniel E. Koshland, Jr., the new editor of *Science*, wrote in defense of a new design touch on the cover of his journal (a dot over the capital I [!]), "It symbolizes imagination and the willingness of scientists to battle conformism, for these lie at the heart of all great science" (Koshland 1986). A heavy burden for a modest dot to bear, where larger men have failed.

His proclamation impels us to a number of questions: Is it not clear, then, that "great science" is *not* being done, at least in the categories of science that have implications for human behaviors and characteristics? Is it not clear that, once again — or rather, *still* — for the field of science, women and issues of gender remain utterly and profoundly invisible, except to feminists? The "imagination and willingness to battle conformism" to patriarchal gender ideologies, convictions, and stereotypes in scientific theory and practice clearly fall outside the category of unacceptable bias. As one reviewer of my manuscript submitted to *Science* wrote, "While many of Bleier's points in 'Science and Social Values: Research on Sex Differences' are valid, she tends to err in the opposite direction from the researchers whose results and conclusions she criticizes. While Bleier states, toward the end of her paper, that she does not 'deny the possibility of biologically based structural or functional differences in the brain between women and men,' she argues very strongly for the predominant role of environmental influences." That is, there is only one direction in which one may err and still be published in *Science* and other journals,

* Parts of this chapter were included in a paper delivered at the annual meeting of the American Association for the Advancement of Science (AAAS) on February 17, 1987, at the Symposium, *Gender Bias in Sex Differences Research.*

since clearly those studies I had criticized for their sloppy methods, inconclusive findings, and unwarranted interpretations and conclusions about the biological determinants of human behaviors, *had all been published* in *Science* and elsewhere — and, of course, continue to be published.

It is my contention that, despite its editorial proclamation of dedication to the battle against conformism, *Science*, in fact, suppresses dissent. It is closed to those who truly question established scientific orthodoxy (in this case, the dominant paradigm of a biological basis for presumed gender differences in cognitive abilities) no matter how firm their experimental data or cogent their arguments, while it uncritically welcomes scientific, ideological orthodoxy that supports the dominant paradigm, no matter how shoddy the data and tenuous the interpretations. I shall document this charge in the course of this chapter.

The problem of unacknowledged ideological commitments on the part of editors and reviewers is further compounded in the case of *Science* by a new editorial policy initiated by Koshland at the time of his ascent to editordom. As first announced in his editorial of 18 January 1985, he maintains an autocratic exclusionary editorial policy that permits *no* resubmissions, no appeals or refutations of arbitrary publication decisions or of downright ignorant and blatantly biased reviews. To my knowledge *Science* is alone among scientific journals in forbidding responses from authors.

There is another characteristic of the review process of scientific articles that is taken for granted by scientists, but not widely known though perhaps of some interest to non-scientists. None of the reviewing for science journals is blind to the author's identity. In contrast to other disciplines that acknowledge the possibility of personal and professional biases on the part of reviewers that could affect their "objective" judgments about manuscripts, scientists believe that the identity of the investigator and the actual site of the study (the laboratory and the institution) are *themselves* not simply valid factors to consider but essential information implicit in the process of "objectively" judging the scientific worth, credibility, and significance of any study. The potential consequences of this system are rather obvious. One is that in any field it makes for a potentially closed system that perpetuates and protects dominant or mainstream paradigms against any methodological or theoretical challenges. Another is that unacceptably flawed studies are published and then uncritically welcomed into the canon only because of the name and prestige of the senior author. Another is that the work of those who challenge dominant paradigms may be discounted and go unpublished and, thus, come to constitute the suppressed body of negative evidence the apparent absence of which is interpreted as constituting support for the dominant paradigm. When the same incestuous processes hold also for the peer reviewing of proposals for grant funds, without which research in science is virtually impossible, the consequences for *all* fields of science — not only those under consideration here — may be far greater than we can imagine, since it is difficult to imagine the scientific "knowledge" that could or would exist were the premises, approaches, and routes to scientific knowledge different than they have been.

Around the time Koshland became the editor of *Science* I submitted a review article describing conceptual, methodological, and interpretive flaws in several important and widely accepted areas of gender-differences research. I critically analyzed a number of studies in which the authors claimed to demonstrate either the effects of testosterone in determining complex human social behaviors and characteristics or sex differences in brain structure underlying presumed sex differences in cognitive functions. (Much of the contents of the paper submitted to *Science* appears as Chapter 7 in R. Bleier, 1986.) One reviewer recommended publication, the other reviewer was concerned, as quoted above, that my erring "in the opposite [i.e., wrong] direction" was too grievous to permit publication in *Science*, an opinion that evidently the editor was happy to accept.

Before detailing *Science*'s record and my encounters with its editors on the issue of the existence of biological bases for presumed cognitive gender differences, it is necessary briefly to provide the theoretical framework for the controversy.

In recent years there has been intense interest in finding gender differences in brain structure and function to explain presumed gender-related differences in cognitive ability. The focus has been mainly on the question of hemispheric lateralization of cognitive functions, particularly the processing of visuospatial information. (The two hemispheres of the brain are the large, most visible, surface-convoluted parts of the brain where complex, conscious, associative cognitive processing takes place; they are the embodiments of "right brain–left brain" theorizing.) Visuospatial ability is seen as especially critical for success in the areas — science, mathematics, engineering, and a myriad others — that are seen as and have been male domains. The dominant theory holds that males process visuospatial information predominantly with the right hemisphere while females (i.e., girls and women) are said to use both hemispheres more symmetrically. In the absence of any evidence whatsoever, this dominant theory *assumes*, for obvious reasons, that right hemispheric lateralization of the processing of visuospatial information is superior to bilateral hemispheric processing of such information.

A major problem in the enterprise of finding biological bases in the brain for presumed gender differences in cognitive abilities or in hemispheric lateralization of cognitive processes is that the existence itself of such differences is questionable and highly controversial, as at least five recent reviews document in great detail (Alper 1985; Caplan et al. 1985;

Fairweather 1976; Kimball 1981; McGlone 1980).   They show that the body of literature on gender differences in spatial ability is seriously flawed by findings of marginal, if any, statistical significance; by conflicting results and failures of replication; by poor experimental design and lack of sufficient controls for variables; and by a lack of consensus in defining the term "spatial ability." There is little evidence that "spatial ability" is a unitary skill or concept rather than a complex of elements, nor is there any demonstration of what the myriad tests of spatial ability are actually testing or of their relationship to each other (Caplan et al. 1985).

Furthermore the reviews demonstrate that as many published studies find no gender differences as do find them and it seems clear that a fair proportion of studies finding no gender differences is never published. Meta-analysis of the body of studies on cognitive gender differences has found that when such differences are found, they account for no more than 1–5% of the population variance and the difference between mean scores is only one-quarter to one-half of a standard deviation (Hyde 1981). The variation within each sex is far greater than the variation between them, and thus makes virtually meaningless the concept of *gender difference*; gender cannot be predicted by knowing a person's score nor can even a range of scores be predicted by knowing a person's gender. In addition, gender differences on a particular test can be eradicated in a single practice session (Caplan et al. 1985). These characteristics of the research constitute a rather shaky basis for the construction of theories of gender differences. In his review of the literature on cognitive sex differences, Hugh Fairweather (1976) concluded, "It must be stressed, finally, that the majority of studies reviewed here and elsewhere are both ill-thought and ill-performed. . . .We cannot pretend that we are testing a theory of sex differences, since at present none can exist" (p. 267). At the end of a book-length review of the literature on sex differences in hemispheric laterality M. Bryden, a respected leader in the field, wrote: "The literature on sex-related differences in lateralization is rife with inconsistencies. . . .To a large extent, one's conclusions rest on the choice of which studies to emphasize and which to ignore" (1982, p. 238).

The next problem is that, even if there *were* gender-associated differences in hemispheric lateralization of visuospatial function, there is no evidence of a correlation between hemispheric *lateralization* and visuospatial *ability*. It is equally possible that it is superior to process visuospatial information with both hemispheres, and, in fact, Marcel Kinsbourne, another leading worker in the field, suggested (1974) that interhemispheric interaction rather than hemispheric specialization may provide superior intellectual functioning. Roger Sperry, who won a Nobel Prize for his work on hemispheric lateralization, warned against unwarranted extrapolations from his work concerning the significance of hemispheric specialization of function, "One must caution in this connection that the experimentally observed polarity in right-left cognitive style is an idea in general with which it is very easy to run wild. . . .it is important to remember that the two hemispheres in the normal intact brain tend regularly to function closely together as a unit and that different states of mind are apt to involve different hierarchical and organizational levels or front-back and other differentiations as well as differences in laterality" (1986, p. 12).

We know so little about the structural and functional substrates of thinking, consciousness, intelligence, mathematical or musical or verbal ability *in general*, or about how and where they are organized in the cortex, that there is no scientific rationale for a *specific* theory of either hemispheric lateralization of or gender differences in intellectual functioning. Yet we are not wanting for studies that claim to have found *the* structural basis in the brain for presumed gender differences in some cognitive ability.

In 1982 Geschwind and Behan reported an association between left-handedness, certain disorders of the immune system, and some developmental learning disabilities, such as dyslexia and stuttering, a complex more common in boys than in girls. Assuming that left-handedness indicates right hemispheric dominance (because, in general, the right side of the brain communicates with the left side of the body), Geschwind, a well-known neurologist at Harvard, used the study to formulate a general theory to explain the genesis of right-hemispheric dominance in males and, therefore, of course, of gender differences in cognitive abilities. The authors cited a study of human fetal brains (Chi et al. 1977), reporting that two convolutions of the right hemisphere appear one or two weeks earlier during fetal development than their partners on the left. Geschwind and Behan then proposed that testosterone, secreted by the fetal testes, has the effect *in utero* of slowing the development of the left hemisphere, resulting in right-hemispheric dominance in males. The authors failed to mention some profound problems with their theory: there is no evidence for such an inhibiting effect of testosterone on cortical development; it is difficult to imagine how testosterone circulating in the blood stream could selectively affect not only the left hemisphere alone, but only two convolutions on the left side. Far more serious, however, is their failure to mention that Chi and his colleagues specifically stated that they found *no sex differences* in the 507 fetal brains they examined. That finding alone completely undermines Geschwind's theory, since, if testosterone had such an effect, the female fetal brains would not have shown a lag in the development of the two convolutions on the left side. But only a highly skeptical reader of the Geschwind and Behan paper would bother, as I did, to find and to read the Chi et al. article, and thus discover the crucially withheld information.

Yet *Science*, presumably cautious and rigorous, hailed the new theory of testosterone-directed, gender-differentiated brain development (unencumbered as the theory was by any plausible data whatsoever, it qualifies as an "elegant" theory explaining *everything*) with the bold headline, "Math Genius May Have Hormonal Basis," for an interview with Geschwind in which he stated that testosterone effects on the fetal brain can produce "superior right hemisphere talents, such as artistic, musical, or mathematical talent" (Kolata, 1983, p. 1312).

Equally pleased was another investigator, Camilla Benbow, who had earlier published a paper concluding that boys have an "endogenous" (i.e., innate) superiority in mathematical ability (Benbow and Stanley, 1980). Benbow, one of a handful of women scientists dedicated to uncovering the biological bases for gender differences (i.e., female inferiority) in cognitive functioning [through their own accomplishments, of course, they demonstrate their own exceptionality, their immunity from biological cognitive infirmity], used the forum of the AAAS (American Association for the Advancement of Science, parent organization to *Science*) annual meeting in 1986 to endorse the wildly speculative testosterone theory. She was quoted as saying that her "data are only consistent with one biological hypothesis, and that is the early hormonal exposure hypothesis" (Madison, *Capital Times*, 27 May, 1986). Her remarks were carried nationwide by the Associate Press and in Madison, Wisconsin, at least, made front-page banner headlines, "Study shows male hormones multiply boys' math skills," a remarkable transformation even of Benbow's claims since her study only tabulated SAT (Scholastic Aptitude Test) math scores for seventh-grade boys and girls and did not, could not, examine testosterone effects.

A second study reported in *Science* what was claimed to be the first reliable evidence for a sex difference in human brain morphology, a larger and more bulbous *splenium* of the *corpus callosum* in women (de Lacoste-Utamsing and Holloway, 1982). The *corpus callosum* is in the brain of all mammals and is a sheet of nerve fibers (which are *axons*, the long processes of neurons that make functional connections with other neurons in the transmission of information) connecting the two hemispheres. Viewed from the midline (see Figure 3) the callosum is a clearly delineated structure and the portion toward the back of the brain is known as the *splenium*.

The study was based on only 14 brains (9 male, 5 female) obtained at autopsy, with no specification of age of patients, cause of death, or mode of selection of the particular 14 brains from all available autopsy specimens. These important methodological questions were particularly troublesome for three reasons. First, the authors stated that they undertook measurements of the callosum *after* the "serendipitous" observation, in the course of examining many brains for other purposes, of a sex difference in the shape of the *splenium*. Second, the reported distribution of values for splenial maximum width for males and females was completely bimodal, i.e., mutually exclusive, a statistical improbability for any biological

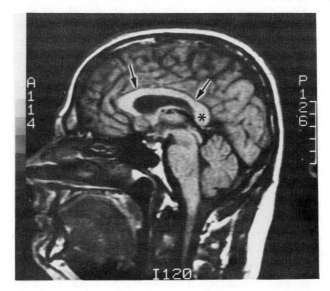

Fig. 3. A magnetic resonance image of a human head. The view is of the
midline. The corpus callosum is indicated by arrows and the splenium by an
asterisk. The subject is an adult male; his splenium is large and bulbous.

parameter (except reproductive) in *randomly* selected populations of
males and females. Finally, the authors attributed "wide-ranging implications for students of human evolution, as well as for neuropsychologists in
search of an anatomical basis for possible gender differences in the degree
of cerebral lateralization" (p. 1431), even though the reported sex
difference in the area of the posterior fifth, defined by the authors to be
representative of the splenial surface area, was not statistically significant
(P=0.08).

Furthermore, the authors made the assumptions, for which there is no
evidence, that size of *splenium* reflects the number of *axons* passing
through it and is directly related to the degree of symmetry of hemispheric
functioning. Thus, on the basis of a series of unsupported assumptions, the
authors speculate that their "results are congruent with a recent neuro-
psychological hypothesis that the female brain is less well lateralized —
that it manifests less hemispheric specialization — than the male brain for
visuospatial functions." With the suggestive phrasing, "less hemispheric
specialization," the authors leave it to the reader to draw the obvious
implication that they have found the biological basis for the presumed
inferiority of girls and women for visuospatial functions.

With all of its basic scientific flaws, an unstated methodology in sample
selection and an unacceptable sample size, unsupportable assumptions
leading to overblown interpretations, a "finding" without a minimum
standard of statistical acceptability, *Science* found this paper important

enough to publish. One must ask whether it is because Holloway, a leading paleoanthropologist from Columbia University, is one of an inner circle of privileged contributors who need not meet *anyone's* minimum scientific standards; or because he and his co-author reached a conclusion that the editors and reviewers find culturally and socially pleasing no matter how shoddy the evidence or reasoning.

That the flawed methodology of the study produced flawed results is amply demonstrated by the failure of four subsequent studies independently to confirm the finding of a gender-related dimorphism in the *splenium* (Bleier et al. 1986; Demeter et al. 1985; Weber and Weis 1986; Witelson 1985b).

Our own study, based on magnetic resonance images (similar in appearance to x-rays) of 39 subjects (22 female, 17 male), repeated all of the measurements made by de Lacoste-Utamsing and Holloway and added several other parameters. As stated above we found no gender-associated differences in the *splenium* and in our paper we discussed the impossibility, in light of what is known today about the *corpus callosum* and cognitive functions in general, of correlating callosal size or shape with any cognitive functions.Nothing is known about the significance, if any, of the enormous individual variations that exist among *corpora callosa*, nor is there any knowledge about the functions of the callosum in cognitive processes.

Furthermore, as I noted once before in this chapter, with all of the insights into how individual neurons process information from the outside world — like sound or light waves — there is a huge and possibly unbridgeable gap between that kind of knowledge and an understanding of such profound questions as how do we think, what are the processes of learning and memory, what is consciousness, what brain processes account for intelligence or for genius or for great ability in math or music. That is, if we had Einstein's or Mozart's brain to analyze, we would not even know what questions to ask of it or where to look or how to go about finding the site of their genius. In the light of this profound ignorance about the most basic elements of human cognition it is utterly ludicrous to claim *any* particular cognitive significance whatsoever for *any* characteristics of the *corpus callosum*. Such efforts directed at the callosum (or any other particular structure in the brain for that matter) are today's equivalent of nineteenth-century craniology: if you can find a bigger bump here or a smaller one there on a person's skull, if you can find a more bulbous *splenium* here or a more slender one there (i.e., a bigger bump or a smaller one) in someone's *corpus callosum*, you will know something significant about their intelligence, their personality, their aspirations, their astrological sign, their gender and race, and their status in society. We are still mired in the naive hope that we can find something that we can *see* and *measure* and it will explain everything. It is silly science and it serves us badly.

We submitted our paper, of course, to *Science*, which, of course, rejected it. One reviewer had no criticisms of the paper and recommended publication as an important addition to this literature. The other reviewer provided a list of six worrisome points not one of which was relevant and answerable and some of which were actually deliberately misleading and false. For example, "We have no idea what size of *corpus callosum* means — more fibers, more glia?" Exactly true, but was s(he) recommending that we call in the subjects and request just a little brain biopsy so we could investigate this point? "Some of the cases apparently had brain pathology." Possibly, but our paper stated that we eliminated all subjects with known brain pathology, and what about the Holloway paper that said *nothing* about the cause of death of their subjects nor about the presence or absence of brain pathology? "While the study criticizes the previous work for small numbers, they have 9/bin average compared with 7/bin and this is not too different." This is deliberately misleading: we had 17 (males) and 22 (females), or an average of *19.5*, not 9 in our male and female categories (bins).

We have, meanwhile, published a paper discussing many of these issues and referring to the results of our study (Bleier et al. 1986), though our primary data have yet to be published. *Science* was similarly unwilling to publish in its letters column my letter outlining the scientific flaws in the de Lacoste-Utamsing and Holloway paper that it had found acceptable to publish. The sad fact is that on the basis of the one deeply-flawed study published in *Science*, this piece of misinformation concerning a gender-associated structural difference in the human brain has been rapidly incorporated into the neuroscientific literature, including its authoritative textbooks, and will not be dislodged for at least a decade. So much for *Science* and the battle against conformism.

BIAS AND PERCEPTION

To conclude this chapter I should like to place this account within the context of how science is ordinarily practiced. Gender (or race or class) is not the only category of bias or viewpoint or subjectivity that affects accepted scientific "knowledge" and practice; it is only the most invisible and unacknowledged. Those familiar with or working within disciplines other than the natural sciences take for granted the varied and contradictory viewpoints that exist among scholars on any given subject, even when sensitive social issues like gender or race are not involved. They know of the intense personal and professional animosities and feuds, the vested interests in one theory or another. What may not be so widely recognized is that the same is true for work within the natural sciences: the widely differing opinions, intense passions, irrational responses, and bitter personal antagonisms. Every scientist has (and was trained within) a distinctive set of scientific and nonscientific viewpoints and assumptions (presuppositions, premises, givens) that determine his/her particular research interests and questions, approaches, methods, interpretations, and conclusions. These are likely to be vastly different and contradictory among researchers working in the exact same area. The same set of data will be accepted or not and be interpreted very differently by different investigators even though the data presumably embody those objective truths of nature we seek to apprehend. This situation is true regardless of the social relevance of the subject.

What this means is that, however rigorously any scientist attempts to be objective when investigating natural phenomenon (i.e., minimizing insofar as possible conscious personal social values, biases, and judgments and avoiding the manipulation of results for preconceived ends), there is an irreducible level of subjectivities in the project, as is true for any human and social production of knowledge. In addition to those related to scientists' training experiences as noted above, the reasons are many and complex.

One is simply that scientists are human and, like everyone else, each has a unique life history as well as specific location with respect to gender, class, race, and ethnicity, and consequently, a set of values, beliefs, viewpoints, needs, and goals. These affect scientists' perceptions and the production of scientific knowledge just as they affect everyone's perceptions and understanding of any moment, event, object, or phenomenon in the world around her. That is, what we "see" or apprehend at any moment, what meaning a moment, event, or object has for us, is complexly determined by our point of view and our background of knowledge (which is in turn complexly determined by our unique store of interpreted memories of interpreted experiences). These layers of subjectivities will affect what a scientist finds interesting and important to investigate, what assumptions she brings to her work, what methods she considers appropriate, what she actually notices or "sees" in her experiments, what she considers valid evidence to be, and how she interprets her data and communicates her conclusions.

Another subjectivity affecting scientific work may be the intellectual infatuation (or let us say commitment) some scientists have for their own ideas and theories. This intellectual infatuation takes on added passion since scientists are rewarded for having their theories be "correct," for doing science successfully, i.e., for having "successful" experiments that produce consistent results and support coherent, acceptable theories, preferably ahead of anyone else. Without such coherent results there are no grants and, therefore, no research, no publications, no tenure. Another compelling subjectivity is that, for some scientific research, the results have obvious implications for social, political, ideological, or economic values and commitments of the investigator. Thus, rather than implications flowing naturally from the results of a study, as might appear to be the case when one reads the author's coherent and logical account of the work, the foreknowledge of these implications can shape the entire research enterprise in any laboratory: the assumptions one chooses to invoke, the evidence that is accepted as valid to consider, the methods used, the interpretations of the data, the well-reasoned conclusions.

These subjectivities that I have listed, and more, affect nearly all the daily scientific activity that occurs anywhere, making it always a partial and contingent expression of what it would otherwise be, skewed and distorted in some particular way by the particular beliefs, needs, and aims of its practitioners. Thus it is more accurate to view scientific knowledge not as synonymous with the objective phenomena it purports to describe, but as sets of beliefs and interpretations that more or less represent a consensus among workers in the field at any particular moment. One is led to conclude that there must be, finally, an irreducible level of distortion or biasing of knowledge production simply because science is a social activity performed by human beings in a specific cultural and temporal context.

Through a detailed examination of two papers that were published in two leading scientific journals, *Science* and *Nature*, Brian Martin (1979) analyzed the multiple sites where bias affects the final conclusions of any scientific study. The two papers were concerned with the effect of exhausts from supersonic transports, such as Concorde, on the upper atmosphere. One paper concluded there is an effect; the other that there is not. Martin begins his argument by stating, "From my point of view, the authors do not disinterestedly look at the available evidence, do not make a balanced analysis, and do not present results in a neutral manner. Rather, it appears to me that the authors from the beginning support or favor a particular conclusion, and in a number of ways organize their scientific work so as to selectively support this conclusion. . . .I believe that the type of analysis made here of [these two] papers could be applied to the work of all scientists to a similar if not greater degree" (p. 25).

First, Martin showed that the two authors, as is necessary for all scientists embarking on a study, made a large number of technical assumptions. Usually quite a few different assumptions can be made, all of which can be justified though only some may turn out to be correct. He showed that both authors chose those assumptions that promoted their conclusions more than would the majority of alternative assumptions. Next, Martin pointed out that scientists must draw evidence from a number of sources to develop an argument in support of the hypothesis that is to be (presumably) tested in the study. Since vast amounts of evidence are usually available, the investigator must be selective in the choice of evidence to be considered and presented. Evidence is never neutral; it reflects viewpoints and it needs to be interpreted. Evidence can be found for any viewpoint, so scientists may easily select and interpret evidence to support a particular viewpoint and the conclusion reached by the study, as did the authors of both studies. Next, Martin found that both authors pushed their arguments by selectively using only those experimental results that favored their own case, ignoring contradictory findings, and in the *abstracts* and *summary* sections (the parts of a paper selectively read by the majority of journal readers), dropping the qualifying phrases that scientific accuracy required in describing their results in the body of the paper.

In the context of his discussion of literary works, in particular realist fiction, where the reader's attention is drawn not to the "act of enunciating," to *how* something is said, but rather to *what* is said, Terry Eagleton (1983) makes a comparison with the scientific text that succinctly described the problems Martin has described:

> The language of a legal document or scientific textbook may impress or even intimidate us because we do not see how the language got there in the first place. The text does not allow the reader to see how the facts it contains were selected, what was excluded, why these facts were organized in this particular way, what assumptions governed this process, what forms of work went into the making of the text, and how all of this might have been different. (p. 170).

If I were to broaden even further the context for this chapter within the general practice of science, it would be necessary to consider a range of social, political, and economic factors that influence, if not virtually determine, the directions of scientific research, what research is actually done, and, thus, what constitutes the existing body of scientific knowledge. Such analysis is properly the province of the sociology of science and would itself constitute a lengthy text that is beyond the intent of this chapter. It would have to consider such questions as why certain research is done and not others, who defines what are important research directions, who controls the funding of research, who does research, who benefits, who judges the worth of research that is done, etc. (see Brian Martin, 1979* for a detailed discussion of these issues).

Thus one can say that the techniques and flaws of gender-differences research in the neurosciences described in this chapter represent ordinary, well-practiced techniques common to the conduct of research and the written communication of research results. Several considerations take the bias of gender (like race) out of the realm of the ordinary practice of science. As noted before, it is the most invisible, unacknowledged, and denied bias since it is an implicit part of the androcentric (man-centered) structure, organization, practice, and self-definition of science. Thus unlike the other idiosyncratic passions, differences, and animosities characterizing ordinary scientific activities and discourses, the more generalized and pervasive gender biases and assumptions are *not* out on

---

* For a copy of the monograph, *Bias in Science*, write to Brian Martin, University of Wollongong, P.O. Box 1144, Wollongong, N.S.W. 2500, Australia.

the table to be evaluated along with other viewpoints. The results of gender-biased research have implications for the most cherished and tenaciously held beliefs and stereotypes that structure our society — its families, work force, and institutions, including science itself. Finally, while the ordinary controversies are fuelled mainly by the personal self-interest of individual investigators and the consequences affect mainly themselves, each other, and their research, the consistent and unacknow-ledged biasing in the conduct of gender-differences research has profound consequences for an entire social class — women — who thus far have not participated in the fray and, as a class, have reaped no benefits.

In conclusion I have briefly discussed in this chapter an important area of scientific research that provides scientific, "natural" explanations for the male-structuring of science and for the small proportion of women in the natural sciences, engineering, and mathematics. It produces the scientific bases for the comfortable cultural constructions, the stereotypes, of Woman that make her an unsuitable participant in spheres outside those our patriarchal structures and traditions have defined for her. The results of such studies, however flawed, find easy acceptance by scientists, editors, and reporters alike, who benefit personally and professionally from the perpetuation of gender stereotypes and the traditional structuring of our society, and the scientific "findings" also resonate harmoniously with the ideologies and needs of the larger androcentric society whose scientists produced them.

REFERENCES

Alper, J. S. 1985. Sex differences in brain asymmetry: a critical analysis. *Feminist Studies* **11**: 7–37.

Benbow, C., and Stanley, J. 1980. Sex differences in mathematical ability: Fact or artifact? *Science,* **210**: 1262–1264.

Bleier, R. 1986 (Ed.) *Feminist Approaches to Science.* New York: Pergamon Press.

Bleier, R., Houston, L., and Byne, W. 1986. Can the corpus callosum predict gender, age, handedness, or cognitive differences? *Trends in Neurosciences* **9**: 391–394.

Bryden, M. 1982. *Laterality: Functional Asymmetry in the Intact Brain.* New York: Academic Press.

Caplan, P. J., MacPherson, G. M., and Tobin, P. 1985. Do sex-related differences in spatial abilities exist? *American Psychologist* **40**: 786–799.

Chi, J. G., Dooling, E. C., and Gilles, F. H. 1977. Gyral development of the human brain. *Annals of Neurology* **1**: 86–93.

De Lacoste-Utamsing, C., and Holloway, R. L. 1982. Sexual dimorphism in the human corpus callosum. *Science* **216**: 1431–1432.

Demeter, S., Ringo, J., and Doty, R. W. 1985. Sexual dimorphisms in the human corpus callosum. Abstr. *Society for Neuroscience* **11**: 868.

Eagleton, T. 1983. *Literary Theory.* Minneapolis: University of Minnesota Press.

Fairweather, H. 1976. Sex differences in cognition. *Cognition* **4**: 231–280.

Geschwind, N., and Behan, P. 1982. Left-handedness: association with immune disease, migraine, and developmental learning disorder. *Proceedings of National Academy of Sciences* **79**: 5097–5100.

Hyde, J. S. 1981. How large are cognitive gender differences? A meta-analysis using w^2 and d. *American Psychologist* **36**: 892–901.

Kimball, M. M. 1981. Women and science: a critique of biological theories. *International Journal of Women's Studies* **4**: 318–338.

Kinsbourne, M. 1974. Mechanisms of hemispheric interaction in man. In M. Kinsbourne and L. Smith (Eds.), *Hemispheric Cerebral Function*. Springfield, IL: Charles Thomas.

Kolata, G. 1983. Math genius may have hormonal basis. *Science* **222**: 1312.

Koshland, D. E. 1986. A new look. *Science* **231**: 9.

Martin, B. 1979. *The Bias of Science*. Marrickville, Australia: Southwood Press.

McGlone, J. 1980. Sex differences in human brain asymmetry: a critical survey. *The Behavioral and Brain Sciences* **3**: 215–263.

Sperry, R. 1986. Consciousness, personal identity, and the divided brain. In M. F. Lepore, M. Ptito and H. H. Jasper (Eds.), *Two Hemispheres — One Brain*. New York: Alan R. Liss.

Weber, C., and Weis, S. 1986. Morphometric analysis of the human corpus callosum fails to reveal sex-related differences. *J. Hirnforschungen* **27**: 237–240.

Witelson, S. 1985b. The brain connection: the corpus callosum is larger in left-handers. *Science* **229**: 665–668.

Chapter 6

The Impact of Feminism on the AAAS Meetings: From Nonexistent to Negligible

Sue V. Rosser

For years I have always felt an outsider at national professional meetings in either science or women's studies. At the science meetings. I was usually the only, or one of a very small group of feminists interested in feminist questions and/or critiques of science. At women's studies meetings I was usually one of a very small group of scientists interested in scientific questions within feminism.

Back in the 1970s, although it was lonely, I didn't find this position very surprising. After all, this phase of the women's movement was rather new. Women's health and reproductive rights, which might in some ways be viewed as applied science, were two of the major issues that catalyzed the rebirth of the movement in the 60s and 70s. These areas became issues partially because there were very few women in decision-making positions in health care or basic science.

However, women's studies, the academic arm of the women's movement, grew during the decade of the 1970s from essentially no formal programs and a few scattered courses to 452 programs and over 30,000 courses (Howe 1984). Concurrently, during the 1970s statistical data indicate that more women were entering scientific fields. For example in *Technology Review,* Hornig (1984) reported that nearly 4,500 women earned Ph.D.s in science and engineering compared with 1,500 in the humanities. Between 1973 and 1983 women as a percentage of life science post-doctorates went from 21.5 to 32% (Filner 1986).

If these statistics were accurate why then was I not finding more feminists at scientific meetings and more scientists at women's studies meetings? Furthermore, if so many more women were earning Ph.D.s in scientific fields than in the humanities, why did I have the impression that women's studies and feminist scholarship were having more of an impact upon the theories and methodologies of the humanities disciplines than they were upon the sciences? One of my women's studies colleagues in English had told me that about half of the papers at her major national professional meeting were on feminism or women's issues. Were all the women in the humanities feminists and all the women in the sciences non-feminists? Surely not.

I was aware that part of the answer to these questions was that there were and still are not very many women in science. Although Vetter's statistics (1981) indicate that more women have received advanced degrees in science and engineering in the 1970s and 1980s than in the 1950s and 1960s, the 1986 Report of the National Science Foundation documents that many fewer women (10.7%) than men (89.3%) receive degrees in sciences and engineering (exclusive of the social sciences where women comprise 34.6% of the population). The salaries, promotion, and advancement rates of women scientists are lower than those of men scientists at all ranks (except in engineering) and unemployment rates for women are higher (NSF, 1986). In the ten-year interval 1975–84 women went from 16.9% of NIH study section members to only 17.9%; during this time the total number of members doubled from 733 to 1,264 (Filner 1986). The National Academy of Sciences, which has a membership of 2,610, has had only 57 women members elected since the Academy was chartered in 1863 (Rubin 1986). Almost all of them were elected within the last decade. Thus the women who are in science, particularly those at the higher ranking positions, still find themselves in the vast minority.

Because of their minority position most women fear, and rightly so, that any commitments such as those to women's studies will make them appear more peripheral to traditional science and thus lessen their chances for promotion and tenure. The documented discrimination against women in science (Vetter 1980) and the perception of many scientists that good science requires that all of one's energy and thought processes be directed towards pursuing the problem in the laboratory substantiate their fears about the effects that involvement with anything outside of science (including women's studies) might have on their careers.

When one converts the raw numbers to percentages and takes into consideration the barriers against the women in science it seems less surprising that feminists have not had more impact upon the scientific disciplines. But some feminists in science have been busy producing a new scholarship on women. Springing from the roots of work done in the late 1960s and early 1970s feminists in the 1980s have produced a flowering of scholarship on women and science. This scholarship might be grouped into five different but related categories:

1. The history of women in science: Using some of the methods developed by feminist historians, Margaret Rossiter (1982) in *Women*

Scientists in America provides the prototype of work to recover the names of and information about the daily lives of past women in science.

2. Feminist critiques of science: Beginning with the work by Ruth Hubbard and Marian Lowe, *Women Look at Biology Looking at Women* (1979) and continued by Ruth Bleier, *Science and Gender* (1984) and Janet Sayers, *Biological Politics: Feminist and Anti-feminist Perspectives,* (1982) feminists have sought to expose the flaws in research design, subject choice, data interpretation, and theoretical constructs in much of the current research that purports to demonstrate a biological basis for female inferiority.

3. Current status of women in science: Two types of work provide insight into the daily lives of women currently working in science. In *A Feeling for the Organism* by Evelyn Fox Keller (1983), *Rosalind Franklin and DNA* by A. Sayre (1975), and *Women in Science* by Vivian Gornick (1983) the authors demonstrate the struggles, triumphs, and defeats of individual women scientists. The other type of work—for example, the *1986 NSF Report on Women and Minorities in Science and Engineering,* and *Women in Scientific and Engineering Professions* by Violet Haas and Carolyn Perucci (1984)— reports statistical information and survey results that explore educational, professional, and employment opportunities and obstacles for women in science.

4. Feminist theory of science: While all categories defined here indirectly attempt to suggest what theoretical differences would exist between a feminist science and a nonfeminist science, only Evelyn Fox Keller in *Reflections on Gender and Science,* (1985), devotes much space to dealing directly with the question.

5. Feminist curriculum transformation in the sciences: Probably the most recent area to surface involves taking the information gathered from the other four categories of research and incorporating it, along with some feminist pedagogical methods, into the science classroom and curriculum. Several cross-disciplinary works, such as Marilyn Schuster and Susan Van Dyne's *Women's Place in the Academy* (1985) have included chapters on science curricula; my own work (1986) *Teaching Science and Health from a Feminist Perspective* falls into this category.

However, I questioned the extent to which this information was reaching "mainstream" scientists. The scientist in me wanted to see some data that might shed light on this question of the impact of women's studies on the scientific disciplines. This is what led me to undertake this study.

I collected data from three different sources:

First, I examined the programs of the American Association for the

S. V. ROSSER

Advancement of Science (AAAS), the major national multi-disciplinary scientific organization, for the last 20 years. In order to determine whether or not there had been an increase in papers relating to women's studies or feminism over time, I counted the number of papers presented in two ways: those that centered on women's studies or feminist issues and those that were of general concern to women in any way. It should be noted that I did not count papers dealing with children or children's health under either category; however I did of course count papers dealing with pregnancy, childbirth, or lactation under the second category. Basically, I was very generous in including papers that contained any information of interest to women. Thus I would consider these data to represent an overestimate of the number of papers relating to women's issues or feminism within the AAAS.

TABLE 6.1. *AAAS*

Year	Category One Papers of general concern to women		Category Two Papers on feminist issues	
	Number	*Percentage*	*Number†*	*Percentage†*
1965	47/1313	3.6%	13/1313	1.8 %
1966	16/683	2.3%	5/683	.7%
1967	3/135	2.2%	0/135	0%
1968	4/179	2.2%	4/179	2.2%
1969	11/156	7.0%	4/156	2.6%
1970	6/132	4.5%	1/132	.76%
1971	15/130	11.5%	8/130	6.2%
1972	27/582	4.5%	6/93	6.4%
*1973				
1974	6/128	4.7%	6/128	4.7%
1975	10/122	8.2%	4/122	3.3%
1976	7/177	4.0%	6/177	3.4%
1977	5/122	4.1%	3/122	2.5%
1978	3/136	2.2%	2/136	1.5%
1979	7/135	5.2%	6/135	4.4%
1980	2/139	1.4%	2/139	1.4%
1981	3/147	2.0%	2/147	1.4%
1982	7/163	4.3%	4/163	2.4%
1983	9/151	6.0%	4/151	2.6%
1984	15/184	8.2%	9/184	4.9%
1985	10/164	6.1%	8/164	4.9%
1986	12/170	7.1%	3/170	1.8%

*Note: The table shows no data from 1973. In that year AAAS switched from a winter (December) to a spring (February) meeting.
†Papers on feminist issues are also included in the number and percentage of papers of general concern to women.

The results of the AAAS data are shown in Figures 4 and 5 and in Table 6.1. It is evident that there has been an increase over the years both in papers of general concern to women in any way (graph 1) from 2.3% in 1966 to 7.1% in 1986 and in papers centering on women's studies or feminist issues (graph 2) from 0.7% in 1966 to 1.8% in 1986. But it is quite clear that neither category has ever represented a large percentage (never more than 11.5%) of the total number of papers at the meeting. Perhaps an even more disturbing trend is the evidence that the number of papers in either category has not peaked in recent years. In fact the peak for both was the early 1970s. In 1971, 11.5% of the papers were of general concern to women and, in 1972, 6.4% were on women's studies or a feminist issue. The numbers in recent years have fluctuated, but have been less encouraging.

Secondly, I examined the programs of the National Women's Studies Association, NWSA, the major national women's studies organization, since its origin in 1979. In order to determine whether or not there had been an increase in papers relating to basic science, mathematics, or health

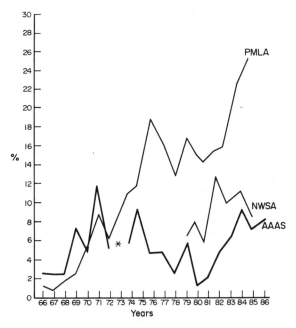

FIGURE 4. Percentages of individual papers during the last two decades.
MLA, the Modern Language Association
AAAS, the American Association for the Advancement of Science
NWSA, the National Women's Studies Association
*Note that in 1973 the AAAS has no data since it switched its meeting time from December to the spring.

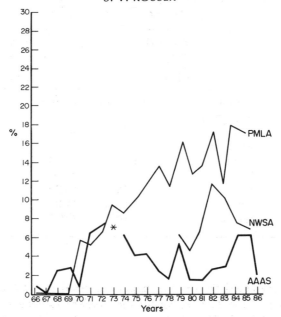

FIGURE 5. Percentages of entire sessions during the last two decades.
MLA, the Modern Language Association
AAAS, the American Association for the Advancement of Science
NWSA, the National Women's Studies Association
*Note that the AAAS data represent individual papers dealing with feminist or women's
studies issues. Also note absence of data for 1973.

issues over that period of time, I counted the papers in two ways:
individual papers relating to science, math or health issues and entire
sessions relating to science, math or health issues.

Ironically, the NWSA data show a remarkable similarity to the AAAS
data. (Please note that starting with 1979 does cut off the peak years for
women-related and feminist papers at AAAS.) As you can see from
Figures 4 and 5 and Table 2 up until 1986 the percentage of papers has
ranged from 5.8% to 11.7%, and the percentage of entire sessions has
ranged from 4.1% to 10.1%. In 1986 the percentage of individual papers is
16.77% and of entire sessions is 14.07%. These 1986 data represent the
highest percentages during the 8-year period. In 1986 the title of the
NWSA conference was Women Working for Change: Health, Culture and
Societies. But even when health is one of the three foci of the conference
less than 17% of the papers are on science, health or mathematics.

The NWSA and AAAS data did seem to confirm my hunch. Feminist
scientific papers always seemed to constitute less than 17% of papers at
AAAS and NWSA conferences. But this data did not shed any light upon
the relationship between feminism and the humanities.

TABLE 6.2. *NWSA*

	Category One Individual papers on science, health, or mathematics		Category Two Entire sessions on science, health, or mathematics	
Year	Number	Percentage	Number	Percentage
1979	20/341	5.9%	11/206	5.3%
1980	38/557	6.8%	10/246	4.1%
1981	19/345	5.5%	12/211	5.7%
1982	46/392	11.7%	15/149	10.1%
1983	52/612	8.5%	21/238	8.8%
1984	57/590	9.7%	19/270	7%
1985	39/543	7.2%	14/246	5.7%
1986	113/674	16.77%	38/270	14.07%

Thirdly, I examined the titles of papers as listed in the Preconvention Program Issue of the *Proceedings of the Modern Language Association* (PMLA) for 1965–85. The Modern Language Association is the largest multidisciplinary national organization for humanities disciplines and in that sense is comparable to the AAAS for science disciplines. The individual papers on feminist or women's issues were counted. These data are comparable to category one of the AAAS data. Data that would be comparable to category two of the AAAS data were not counted since the category would have included most of the papers at the meeting. (Many papers dealt with female characters, literary themes such as love, or authors such as Jane Austen, long accepted in the male literary tradition. Although these papers were of general interest to women they consititute a very large percentage of the papers.)

In contrast to the AAAS and NWSA data on feminism and science, the MLA data indicate a steady increase in the number of individual papers and entire sessions devoted to feminism and women's issues over the last 20 years. Beginning in 1967, 0.72% of the individual papers and 0% of the entire sessions were devoted to feminism; by 1985 24.22% of the individual papers and 16.61% of the entire sessions were on women's issues. The black lines on Figures 4 and 5 and Table 6.3 demonstrate the increasing impact of women's studies and feminism on the national meeting.

RESULTS

The results of the AAAS data are shown in Table 6.1 and those of the MLA data in Table 6.3. The figures and tables demonstrate that there has been an increase over the years in the papers on feminist or women's issues

presented at the annual meetings of both the AAAS and MLA. Papers
centering on women's studies or feminist issues at AAAS meetings have
increased from 0.7% in 1966 to 1.8% in 1986. In 1966, 1.17% of the papers
at MLA focused on these issues; in 1985 the percentage was 24.22%. The
percentage of papers presented at the AAAS meetings on feminist and
women's studies has increased during the past two decades. However, it has
increased significantly less ($t = -5.13$; significant at the 0.0001 level)
during the same time period than the percentage of papers on such issues at
the MLA.

The peak of papers on feminist and women's studies issues at AAAS did
not occur in the 1980s but in 1971. In contrast the papers on feminist issues
represented a smaller percentage of the total number of papers at the MLA
than the AAAS in the late 1960s. However, beginning in 1972 the
percentage of feminist or women's studies papers at MLA surpassed that at
AAAS. The percentage presented at MLA increased steadily with the
highest percentage occurring in 1985 when 24.22% of the papers were on

TABLE 6.3. *PMLA*

Year	Category One Individual papers on women's studies or feminist issues		Category Two Entire sessions on women's studies or feminist issues	
	Number	*Percentage*	*Number*	*Percentage*
1966	3/256	1.17%	0/111	0
1967	2/276	0.72%	0/131	0
1968	5/293	1.71%	0/140	0
1969	7/311	2.25%	0/155	0
1970	18/321	5.61%	9/168	5.36%
1971	32/379	8.44%	9/175	5.14%
1972	23/388	5.93%	14/224	6.25%
1973	39/464	8.40%	25/282	8.86%
1974	72/674	10.68%	27/337	8.01%
1975	124/1101	11.26%	51/524	9.73%
1976	246/1340	18.36%	74/636	11.64%
1977	177/1190	14.87%	90/699	12.88%
1978	126/1028	12.26%	65/632	10.28%
1979	184/1144	16.08%	94/594	15.82%
1980	136/949	14.33%	53/473	11.20%
1981	170/1280	13.28%	77/634	12.14%
1982	190/1315	14.45%	104/648	16.05%
1983	240/1621	14.81%	68/640	10.60%
1984	405/1814	22.33%	104/612	16.99%
1985	412/1701	24.22%	99/596	16.61%

feminist or women's studies issues. The structural organization of the national meeting may be a factor that partially contributes to the percentage differences between the two organizations. In the late 1960s and early 1970s both the AAAS and the MLA underwent an evaluation of their organization and annual meeting. Before that time the annual meetings of both organizations had been a somewhat unwieldy conglomeration of the individual meetings of the many societies that made up each organization. Over a several-year period the AAAS and MLA each studied and changed the organization of its annual meeting.

Although the reasons for the study and change may have been similar in the two organizations the results were quite different. The AAAS "tightened" the hierarchical structure of its meeting, sharply reducing the total number of papers and sessions presented. For example, in 1965 the total number of papers was 1,313; by 1971 the total number of papers had been reduced to 130. The latter number has remained fairly steady throughout the late 1970s and early 1980s. In contrast the MLA permitted the number of papers to increase steadily, although most sessions were no longer sponsored by a specific society. Thus in 1966, 256 individual papers were presented at MLA; by 1971 the number had increased to 379. Steadily increasing, the number of papers presented reached 1,701 at the 1985 MLA convention. Perhaps the looser structure and increased number of papers at MLA permitted more feminist topics to be presented than the tighter structure with fewer papers of AAAS. The NWSA data (Table 6.2) fall between that of the AAAS and the PMLA.

CONCLUSIONS AND DISCUSSION

My friend in English studies who suggested that half of the papers at the MLA were now devoted to women's issues was exaggerating. But she had noted a very important trend and the significant impact and acceptance that feminism has had in her discipline. Modern languages do not constitute the only disciplines in the humanities nor is the AAAS the only scientific society. Limited data that I was able to obtain from other professional organizations was not comparable to the AAAS and MLA in terms of size and multidisciplinary range of the organizations. Nor was I able to obtain access to the programs with paper topics of many organizations.

Most professional organizations that have gathered statistics on gender issues have focused their data collection on numbers of women participating in the organization at various levels. For example, the American Mathematical Society reported on the relative numbers of men versus women in several categories: "The general picture is that although women are 13% of the current membership, over the last five years 5% were speakers at special sessions, over the last 10 years 2% were invited hour speakers, and the percentage of women editors has risen from 5% in 1976 to 8% in 1985" (Keen 1986, p. 1). Similarly, in "A Statistical Report on the Participation of Women in the Southern Historical Association, 1935–1985," the historians gathered data on the percentages of women in the Association on the executive council (0–13%), committees (17–19%), program (15–22%), program chairs (10–16%), paper presenters (18–24%), and program commentators (17–23%). During the period from 1975 to 1985 these percentages have increased in every category.

Data demonstrating the participation of women in an association is not comparable to data on the number of papers presented on a feminist or women's studies issue at the national meeting. Thus it is not possible to compare this data directly with that from the MLA, AAAS, and NWSA. Although a higher percentage of women participating in the professional association may lead to more papers on feminist or women's studies issues being presented at the meetings this is not necessarily the case. Many if not most women present papers on traditional and non-feminist topics, just as men may present papers on feminist topics. Thus the impact that feminism or women's studies is having on a field must be gleaned from examining data on the topics of the papers presented, not on the number of women active in the profession.

This helps to explain the paradox of the levels at which the scientific professions continue to resist feminism, even as more women are becoming scientists. Since feminist issues and women's studies papers constitute almost a quarter of the papers being presented at the MLA, they are part of the "mainstream" of the research occurring in the field. An individual doing feminist or women's studies research in the modern languages is mainstream and need not greatly fear that her work will be branded as peripheral or marginal to the field, thus lessening her chances for promotion and tenure.

In contrast feminist and women's studies papers usually constitute less than 5% of papers at the AAAS meetings. Such papers are not part of the "mainstream" of science. Women in science have ascertained correctly that feminism has had little impact upon their field and that if they present papers on feminist topics or affiliate themselves with women's studies their work is likely to be branded as peripheral. The consequences of working on marginal topics may be dire in terms of grant funding, promotion, and tenure.

Because of these dire consequences many women in science, even some who are feminists, may resist doing feminist work. The relatively small percentage of papers presented at the NWSA on topics related to science, mathematics, or health may partially be accounted for by this factor.

An additional factor exists which may inhibit many scientists who are feminists or potential feminists from doing feminist research and attending NWSA conferences. This factor is the resistance of many feminists and some feminist theory to science. Numerous feminist historians and philosophers of science (Fee 1981; Hein 1982; Keller 1982) have described the extent to which science in our society has become synonymous with a masculine, rational objective approach to the world. Other feminists such as Merchant (1979) and Griffin (1978) have described the parallels between this masculine, dominating approach of science to nature and of men to women. These descriptions have led some feminists to assume naively that the solution is to reject science, rather than trying to conceive better approaches to science. Women scientists love science and recognize the extent to which most aspects of which our twentieth-century society are directly or indirectly influenced by science. They recognize the importance of women having scientific knowledge and participating as scientists as a means of shaping the direction that science takes. Women scientists resist feminists who reject science because they view such feminism as an ostrich-like approach that is unlikely to lead to solutions to today's complicated world problems.

The barriers of resistance between science and feminism and scientists and feminists must be lowered. We need more scientists presenting papers at women's studies meetings and more feminist presentations at AAAS. The impact of feminist work on the humanities has been significant. Those of us in science who despair that feminism has had no impact upon our discipline are exaggerating. Unfortunately, the exaggeration is slight and the resistance is great. The effect of women's studies upon science has been a change from non-existent to negligible. We must lower barriers to resistance further if we hope to create a feminist science.

REFERENCES

Bleier, R. 1984. *Science and Gender*. New York: Pergamon Press.

Fee, E. 1981. Is feminism a threat to scientific objectivity? *International Journal of Women's Studies* 4 No. 4: 213–233.

Filner, B. 1986. President's Remarks. *AWIS*, Vol. XV, No. 4, July/August.

Gornick, V. 1983. *Women in Science: Portraits from a World in Transition*. New York: Simon and Schuster.

Griffin, S. 1978. *Women and Nature*. New York: Harper and Row.

Haas, V., and Perucci, C. 1984. *Women in Scientific and Engineering Professions*. Ann Arbor: University of Michigan Press.

Hein, H. 1982. Women and Science: Fitting Men to Think about Nature. *International Journal of Women's Studies* 4: 396–377.

Howe. 1984. *Myths of Coeducation*. Bloomington, Indiana: University of Indiana Press.

Hornig, L. 1984. Women in Technology. *Technology Review*, December.

Hubbard, R. and Lowe, M. 1979. *Women Look at Biology Looking at Women*. Boston: Schenkman Publishing Co.

Keen, L. 1986. President's Report. *Association for Women in Mathematics Newsletter* 16, #4, July-August.

Keller, E. F. 1982. Feminism and Science. *Signs: Journal of Women in Culture and Society* 7, No. 3: 589–602.

Keller, E. F. 1983. *A Feeling for the Organism*. San Francisco: W. H. Freeman & Co.

Keller, E. F. 1985. *Reflections on Gender and Science*. New Haven: Yale University Press.

Merchant, C. 1979. *The Death of Nature: Women, Ecology, and the Scientific Revolution.* New York: Harper and Row.

National Science Foundation. 1986. *Women and Minorities in Science and Engineering.* Report 86-301.

Rosser, S. 1986. *Teaching Science and Health from a Feminist Perspective: A Practical Guide.* New York: Pergamon Press.

Rossiter, M. 1982. *Women Scientists in America.* Baltimore: Johns Hopkins University Press.

Rubin, V. 1986. Women's Work: For Women in Science, a Fair Shake is Still Elusive. *Science* **86**, July/August, 58–65.

Sayers, J. 1982. *Biological Politics: Feminist and Anti-Feminist Perspectives.* New York: Tavistock.

Sayre, A. 1975. *Rosalind Franklin and DNA: A vivid view of what it is like to be a gifted woman in an especially male profession.* New York: W. W. Norton & Company, Inc.

Schuster, M. and Van Dyne, S. 1985. *Women's Place in the Academy.* Totowa, N. J. Rowman and Allenheld.

The 1982–84 Southern Historical Association Ad Hoc Committee on the Status of Women in the Southern Historical Association. *The Journal of Southern History,* Vol. LII, No. 2, May 1986, 282–288.

Vetter, B. 1980. Sex discrimination in the halls of science. *Chemical and Engineering News,* March, 37–38.

Vetter, B. 1981. Degree completion by women and minorities in science increases. *Science* **212**, No. 3.

Chapter 7

The Response of the Health Care System to the Women's Health Movement: The Selling of Women's Health Centers

Nancy Worcester and
Mariamne H. Whatley

On a national and international level the women's health movement continues to be extremely active and popular, surviving the many premature obituaries written for the women's movement as a whole. Connections have been made with women who would not have labeled themselves "feminists" and do not necessarily see themselves as participants in the broader women's movement. These women are often active in local campaigns around women's health care, without identifying this involvement as part of a national health movement. Many others do see their role in this movement. A 1977 survey showed that there were over 1,200 groups and tens of thousands of individual women who considered themselves part of the women's health movement.[1] The National Women's Health Network[2], the national organization devoted exclusively to women's health, has a membership of over 20,000, including several hundred organizations representing a constituency of half a million people (Boston Women's Health Book Collective 1984). One does not have to be a radical to see how central health issues are to every woman's life and that the medical system is simply not meeting most women's needs. The women's health movement's critique of the health care system has been

---

[1] This information was obtained from overhead projection notes for a seminar on marketing women's health centers conducted by Sally Rynne, a leading consultant in this area.

[2] National Women's Health Network, 1325 "G" Street, N.W. Washington D.C. 20005. (202)347–1140.

based on the need for *fundamental changes* which would make health care provision more appropriate to women's real needs and accessible to *all* women.

One small but significant part of the women's health movement in the United States was the establishment of feminist health centers. At least 100 such centers in North America have served as models of what feminist health care could offer (Sloane 1985). Because centers grew out of women's groups in the community their diversity reflected the priorities identified by these local groups. Basic to the founding of these centers were the principles that they should be *women-controlled, for* women, *by* women, working to empower women to make informed decisions about their own health care. Feminist health centers encouraged demystification of medical issues, para-medical and self-help contributions to health care, professional accountability, community participation, evaluation, and control, and political activism around issues of women's health.

One of the authors was active in the women's health movement in Britain, where feminists were committed to strengthening the National Health Service. Action had to be directed towards working within the system, trying to make it more responsive to women's needs. While health care activists in the United States often envied the British National Health Service, feminists in Britain were envious of our sisters in the U.S. It seemed that in establishing feminist health centers it was possible to develop real alternatives and models for the future. Wherever we were we had visions of the day when women's health centers would be everywhere, responding to the needs of all women. In our fantasies we might have pictured our local papers carrying full page notices about the women's clinic and the weekly schedule of women's health activities.

Something strange has happened. Those dreams are coming true but in distorted form; the result is not what we had envisioned. New women's health centers are opening up in many cities, with newspapers carrying full page ads for them and listing the next series of women's health seminars. Comparing these ads with our dreams is a bit like looking at a student's notes when the student has missed the point of a lecture. The words are right, but the message is wrong!

COOPTION OF THE WOMEN'S HEALTH MOVEMENT

Those marketing women's health centers in the U.S. are not innocently missing the point. In a language and style that intentionally mimics that of the women's health movement, these centers are being heralded as a most profitable new addition to health care services. The mass marketing of women's health centers can be viewed as the medical establishment's most recent attempt to coopt the women's health movement.

To some extent the medical establishment has ignored the women's health movement when they could. When we could not be ignored the response has been to coopt the movements we started. In the 1970s much of the medical response to the women's health movement was in relation to the issue of childbirth. Women, critical that a normal healthy process had been turned into a medicalized event, worked for women-controlled birthing options including home-births, childbirth without medical intervention, and midwife-assisted deliveries. Hospitals defused the movement against medicalized childbirth by promoting birthing centers which promised the latest technology in a warm, home-like environment. Although these "alternatives" provided superficial changes, they glossed over an unchanged medical-controlled approach to childbirth.

In 1980 Sheryl Ruzek (p. 336) summarized the pattern of the medical profession's response to feminism in the areas of obstetrics and gynecology:

> All challenges and demands for change are initially resisted by most physicians. Over time, changes that do not seriously threaten physicians' professional status, income, or control over medicine are accepted willingly by a vanguard and reluctantly by others, partly in order to keep their clientele. In contrast, changes which *do* seriously threaten medical dominance or which affect the direct material interests of the medical establishment are fought vigorously, often by invoking the power of the state. When repressive measures fail, a final resort is to coopt programs to allow the medical establishment to reassert control over the activity. Again a vanguard of professionals hail the "new ways" (coopted from more radical challengers) as innovative and desirable and gradually carry along their more conservative colleagues.

MARKETING WOMEN'S HEALTH

Ruzek's description is still very applicable in the late 1980s as we see a "vanguard of professionals" hailing a new approach to women's health. This unprecedented interest in women's health has emerged for several reasons. In simple economic terms, not enough people are sick enough for long enough. This, of course, is not true, but new restrictions by the government and insurance companies mean that people have to be pushed through hospitals faster. Therefore, as new sources of income are needed, health care providers, especially hospitals, are searching for untapped markets. As far as women as clients are concerned, not enough women are having enough babies. As more women delay childbearing health care facilities seek ways to attract women earlier.

> "Hospitals have always thought that by providing obstetric services to a woman she would be bonded to them" . . . says Rynne [a leading women's health center consultant] . . . More women are delaying childbirth. Thus, it's vital for hospitals to form an alliance with women long before their first pregnancy, and women's centers are a way to accomplish that (Winning with Women's Centers 1986).

In addition to trying to "bond" young women to their facilities, the medical system is also starting to recognize that there is a growing population of middle-aged and older women. The time is ripe for medical services to start addressing women's health needs outside of those related to childbearing.

This broader interest in women's health is coinciding with a totally new way of marketing health services. A Supreme Court decision four years ago required that the American Medical Association no longer restrict advertising. Previously, virtually all advertising by physicians had been prohibited. Now there are practically no restrictions on health care advertising as long as it is not false or misleading (Folland 1985). It is now as appropriate to advertise hospitals and health services as it is Coca-Cola and Comet.

Health marketing is a rapidly growing field. In 1978 there were only six health marketing executives in the United States. Today there are more than 2000 health consultants telling hospital administrators how to make a profit out of both sickness and health (Jacobs 1986). In a national survey 94% of hospital administrators agreed with the statement "Marketing is a legitimate function of hospitals" (Whittington and Dillon, cited in Folland 1985). Thirty-six per cent of hospital public relations directors see creative advertising as their "greatest need" (Berkowitz et al., cited in Folland 1985).

This is the climate in which women's health is being "discovered." Marketing consultants are saying what the women's health movement has been saying for years: women call upon the health care system more than men and the sexual division of labor means that women are still responsible for other people's health. Through the ears of a hospital administrator this translates as: if you can hook a woman into your services she could bring along her husband, her children, and two sets of parents. Hospitals are discovering what drug companies have long known. Any time you can develop something to sell to normal, healthy women, there is a huge market waiting to be exploited.

WOMEN'S HEALTH CENTERS

In the late 1980s the women's health center serves as a key element in a marketing strategy to attract healthy women. A number of services for women are packaged together and labeled "The Women's Health Center." Even if the center is directly affiliated to a hospital, to avoid a clinical atmosphere it may be located at a distance from the hospital setting. The centers are decorated in ways that are supposed to appeal to women, with pinks and purples the predominant colors. Home-like wallpapers and artworks by women are popular decor. In imitation of feminist health centers, essential components of the new women's health centers include a resource center (at least a bookshelf full of books on women's health topics), an educational program, a wide range of health professionals so as not to appear physician-oriented, and an emphasis on wellness and preventive health care.

Another example of the appropriation of issues identified by the women's health movement is the visibility of women practitioners in the centers. Women have indicated the importance of having health care practitioners they can trust and who show real concern for them (Jensen and Miklovic 1986). There are also many women who prefer women as practitioners, since, at the least, they are more likely to have had similar experiences. Therefore most women's health centers have all women on the staff, including physicians, nurses, educators and nutritionists, though referrals may be to men. One advertisement emphasizes this point very clearly: the photograph shows two women health care practitioners with the caption "We know how you feel." While this is certainly a very positive move in many ways, having women practitioners does not guarantee a particular philosophy. Also the characteristics women find attractive in practitioners can be simulated. One of the real dangers is that the development of a "new bedside manner" will result in manipulative behaviors. As the health activist Virginia Reath points out, "If you can learn how to talk to women, get them to trust you again, then maybe you can do anything you want" (Jacobs 1986, p. 112). The concept of consumer control is essential to the feminist demand for health care by women for women; medical control, even if by women, undermines this goal.

Women's health centers are being opened wherever there is competition between health service providers. Madison, Wisconsin, a city of only 170,000, has had two women's health centers open within a six-month period. There are already at least six such centers in San Francisco. One man plans to open approximately 50 centers on the west coast within the decade (Jacobs 1986). A 1985 *Hospitals* magazine survey found that 40% of hospitals and 54% of larger hospitals planned to add on new or expand existing specialized women's services within a year (Winning with Women's Centers 1986).

It often seems forgotten that these centers were inspired by feminist health centers. Chicago's Illinois Masonic Medical Center's (IMMC) Women's Health Center, which opened in spring 1982, has served as the model being marketed nationally by Sally Rynne, the center's first director. Rynne claimed that the center is the first of its kind in the country and that "IMMC's decision to separate women's health is unique among U.S. hospitals" (McGuinn 1982). Playing on women's dissatisfaction with present health care provision ("the market is so large for women who are looking for alternatives in health services" [Center Targets Women's Health Care Needs 1984]), Rynne promotes the women's health center concept as a profitable alternative within the system. Rynne has identified a number of reasons why the concept should appeal to hospital administrators:

> A women's center can provide a way for a hospital to differentiate itself from its competitors. It enables a hospital to occupy a desirable market "niche" and enhances the hospital's reputation for progressive and innovative health-care approaches (Rynne 1985).

> The center can be an important recruiting mechanism for a hospital because female OB-Gyn physicians are "incredibly in demand" and establishing a center could draw these practitioners to an institution, says Rynne (Winning With Women's Centers 1986).

Gerald W. Mungerson, executive director of IMMC, recognized the value of the women's center as a marketing tool. It offered "one additional way for the system to 'capture the patient' by providing a variety of entry points to it" (Bills 1984). Rynne spells out in detail why this is attractive:

> Women are often referred to the medical center when ancillary tests are needed or when specialty care is required. These women, who come from all parts of the Chicago area, would not be using the services of Illinois Masonic if it were not for the referrals from the Women's Health Resources Center . . . Inpatient revenue from referrals during 1983 totalled $114,000. From October to December 1983, revenue from ancillary test referrals totalled $5,144 and revenues from lab tests totalled $5.779 (Center Targets Women's Health Needs 1984).

It takes more than pink walls to attract women to these new money-makers. With great insight, marketing specialists have discovered that not all women are alike; detailed papers now describe how to appeal to certain population segments of women. A typical example of this is found in a paper by Gilbert Harrell and Matthew Fors (1985, p. 26):

> From a pragmatic stand point, it is suggested that a newly opened health center build an integrated strategic *thrust* designed to *satisfy* particular target segments. (our emphases)

So, once again we have men thrusting around trying to satisfy needs they have identified for women. We have seen many aspects of our lives where this is not appropriate! For the purposes of this paper we will limit ourselves to looking at how men thrusting themselves into the women's health center market may not be fulfilling some of the most urgent needs identified by the women's health movement.

THE POLITICS OF INFORMATION

The politics of information has been a key issue in the critique of the medical establishment. The women's health movement recognized that much of the power of the medical profession has come from their possession and use of knowledge and information not available to most women. Learning, teaching, demystifying, and sharing information has been a crucial, and the most widespread, component of feminist health work.

Proliferating women's health centers have the potential for offering an exciting range of feminist health education. (See Whatley's "Beyond Compliance: Towards a Feminist Health Education," this volume, for an exploration of what feminist education could look like.) Most of the women's health centers attempt to integrate education into the clinical visit, with the waiting room often serving as a women's health library/ information center. There is also usually educational programming to the community on such popular topics as osteoporosis, PMS, reproductive cancers, as well as fitness, nutrition, and stress management. The library and seminars are usually not moneymakers in themselves, but do serve another important function. For example, one center lost money on its seminar series but patient appointments increased by 5% (Bush 1985), so the investment was deemed worthwhile. Another center requires that all attendees at their free evening educational programs be members. Membership hooks them into the center as they receive center newsletters and discounts on center services (Winning With Women's Centers 1986). Others sell their packaged educational programs and/or lists of resources to other centers.

In the marketing strategies established for women's health centers, education plays an important role. Rynne stresses educational programs as part of the public relations component of promotion. She also suggests in her marketing seminars that if the center is at the point at which it can offer only educational programs, then "if well done, [these programs] can hold [the] niche until competition acts further." If many centers are competing in an area, the segmentation approach suggested by Harrell and Fors (1985) can be used in the educational programs. The population is divided into segments with specific characteristics and then the programs are marketed to each specific group; obviously, only segments that have sufficient money are targeted. For example, there may be a fair number of middle-class athletically-active women in the population. Seminars on sports injuries for women, nutritional issues in training, and athletic amenorrhea might attract this segment to the center's services. It is clear from the extensive use of direct mailings, newspaper announcements and newsletters to advertise the educational offerings that the education component is a major marketing strategy of the women's health centers.

For the education component to empower women, it must be a fundamental component in the center and not used simply as a way to get women in the door. It is worrisome to see "how to set up a center" materials emphasizing that the cost of the education component will stabilize after the initial expenditure to start the center. A commitment to a good education program will require a continued financial commitment.

"ALTERNATIVE" WITHIN THE SYSTEM

A key selling point is that women's health centers are presented as an alternative *within the system*. This "alternative" is being offered within a system which serves some women better than others. The United States and South Africa are the only industrialized countries in the world not to have some sort of national health program that ensures at least basic health care provision for everyone. Women who are not served by the present system are exactly those women most in need of new services. Provisions aimed primarily at those already served can only exaggerate the differences between those who have access to quality health care and those who do not. Issues of race, sexual preference, class, and age are some of the factors that affect the quality of health care women receive.

Racism in society is reflected in racism in the health system and in racial inequalities in access to health care. Maternal death rates are five times higher for Blacks than for whites and infant mortality rates are twice as high for Black infants as for white infants (Butler 1983). Although fewer Black women than white women have breast cancer, a higher percentage of Black women with breast cancer die from it. Unless new health centers consciously work to meet the health needs of women of color, they will continue to perpetuate a system which better serves white women.

As with racism, heterosexism in society is mirrored by heterosexism in the health system, so lesbians do not have the same access to quality health care as heterosexual women. At least 40% of lesbians believe that the quality of their health care could suffer if their physician knew of their sexual identity (Smith, Johnson and Guenther 1985). The biggest health problem for lesbians, according to a lesbian health center, "is that they avoid seeking needed and routine care" (Peteros and Miller 1982). Nothing in the marketing literature indicates that women's health centers will be committed to services for this 10% (at least) of women. In evaluating the medical profession's response to feminism, health care for lesbians clearly remains an area in which challenges and demands for change are resisted.

The ability to pay will certainly be a limiting factor in access to women's health centers. At least 15% of the population does not have health insurance at all, while at least 27% of the population has inadequate health insurance or is uninsured for part of the year (Dallek 1985). The figures are even higher for the percentage of women who do not have health insurance. These underinsured/uninsured women and most poor women will not have access to the new services. Poverty is the most basic cause of ill health and early death in this society and women's health centers will do nothing to redress these inequalities.

Older women and differently abled women fare very badly within the present system, but are groups especially in need of good health care. Eighty-five per cent of women over 65 have at least one chronic health problem. Health care expenditures for the elderly are estimated to be 3.5

times greater than for the under-65 population. This means that older women (as a group) spend one-third of their median income on medical costs (Sidel 1986, p. 163). Many poor older women cannot "choose" to take care of their health needs. Twenty per cent of elderly poor in Chicago admitted that they were not able to seek help with medical problems even though they thought they needed medical care (Sidel 1986, p. 163). The survey that produced these figures took place at the same time, in the same city, as the IMMC's women's health center was being promoted as the model for medical response to women's health needs. Medicaid (government health insurance for poor) and Medicare (health insurance for elderly) once offered great potential for providing health care to vulnerable groups. These programs have now been cut so drastically that they make less impact than hoped on access to health care. For example, today Medicare only pays 44% of the health care costs of the elderly (Sidel 1986, p. 163). Services at women's health centers may not even be partially covered by Medicare or Medicaid. These centers could actually exaggerate the problem of inaccessibility to health care. For example, a doctor in Bethpage, New York has found that the cost of setting up a women's health center has limited her ability to accept new Medicaid clients (Jacobs 1986).

Women's health centers are being set up in competitive markets to attract consumers to present facilities. They are not being located in new areas, so they will do nothing to rectify the geographical imbalance in access to health care. Currently 18% of the white population, 24% of Hispanics, and 25% of Blacks must travel more than 30 minutes to their nearest doctor (Dallek 1985).

While copying and exploiting some of the outward appearances of feminist health centers, new women's health centers show little potential for (or possibly interest in) playing a role in moving towards the central feminist goal of making quality health care provision available to *all* women.

MEDICALIZATION OF WOMEN'S LIVES

Feminists have been critical of the ways in which normal, healthy processes such as contraception, pregnancy, and childbirth have been medicalized while real health issues like dysmenorrhea, premenstrual tension, and osteoporosis have been ignored by the health care system. Now that women's health issues have been "discovered," we see an expansion into medicalizing whole new areas of women's lives. There are obvious dangers that the medical profession will be taking control over more aspects of women's lives, that more conditions will be labeled as illness and used against the equality of women, that drugs will be increasingly seen as the solution to new "problems," and in the name of prevention, that more women will be hooked into a medical system that does not meet their needs.

A prime example of the process of medicalization of major aspects of our lives can be seen in Premenstrual Syndrome (PMS), a double-edged sword for women. Because a few women are seriously affected by PMS it is a disgrace that health professionals dismissed it for so long as "all in the mind." Katharina Dalton was viewed as a heroine by many women simply because she took PMS seriously. But medical interest in PMS is proving more dangerous to women than medical ignorance. Just at a time when women are starting to make small inroads towards equality, PMS is receiving great scientific and media attention as a sign of women's biological inferiority. Ellen Goodman of the *Boston Globe* (Psychiatric disorders du jour, 1986) reminds us "We just aren't all that far from raging hormonal-imbalance days." With potential for damaging repercussions PMS has recently been given the status of a psychiatric disorder, labelled as periluteal phase dysphoric disorder, in the appendix of the American Psychiatric Association's "Diagnostic and Statistical Manual" (Psychiatric disorder du jour 1986). Yet research on PMS has been so flawed (i.e., no controls) that very little is actually known about the condition.

The definitions of PMS are so vague and varied that the whole period from ovulation to menstruation gets identified as "premenstrual" and everything from irritability and nervousness to suicidal or criminal behaviors gets labelled as part of the syndrome. Definitions are so broad that any women with premenstrual bloating or a craving for sweets fits the description. In fact all normal menstruating women (and premenopausal women who have had hysterectomies but retain their ovaries) are potential consumers for special PMS clinics. In case women do not identify themselves as having a problem, regular newspaper ads, playing on both women's guilt and responsibility for others, show how PMS can be upsetting for other family members without a woman ever recognizing it.

PMS clinics offer counselling and nutrition information for anyone who can afford it. But even at this stage when little is known about its effectiveness and less is known about its safety, progesterone treatment is commonly offered as the "fix." After two decades of scares and problems with contraceptive pills, DES, and estrogen replacement therapy, it is alarming to see the medicalization of one more aspect of women's lives leading to yet another untested hormonal experiment (Eagan 1983). PMS clinics and PMS counselling in the women's health centers capitalize on a "problem" common, by definition, to most women.

"State of the art" technology offered at women's health centers can also help capture normal, healthy women into the system:

> A women's center is a natural launching pad for many hospital programs. Breast cancer and osteoporosis screening, for example, have a more powerful impact on the marketplace when they are part of a women's center, than do similar services offered in traditional practice settings (Rynne 1985, p. 17).

Osteoporosis is another excellent lure for healthy women, since most women hope to reach the age at which it could be a problem. Osteoporosis has recently become a household word, thanks to huge "education" campaigns by Ayerst Laboratories (manufacturers of Premarin, a popular form of estrogen-replacement therapy) and calcium manufacturers (Dejanikus 1985). These campaigns not only helped calcium sales to reach $166 million in 1986, from $18 million in 1980 (Giges 1986), but also created a climate of fear about the condition. Osteoporosis screening has become a common, expensive offering by women's health centers (Cummings and Black 1986) as they intentionally play on women's fears. While these techniques for measuring bone mass are extremely useful for research purposes, their value for routine screening of all women must be questioned (Whatley and Worcester 1986). While screening can show that bone mass has been lost, screening cannot predict whether or not someone is at risk for osteoporosis (Ott 1986). Osteoporosis is an excellent example of where *prevention* must not be confused with *detection*. On the basis of present information, a woman "at risk" should probably be given dietary advice and encouragement to exercise to prevent osteoporosis. All women would benefit from this advice. Therefore, unreliable but sophisticated screening has little value to the consumer at this stage. Requiring regular monitoring of bone mass, osteoporosis screening offers enormous potential for clinics as a profitable procedure and enormous risk to women that estrogen replacement therapy will be seen as a medical dose of prevention.

An additional point on osteoporosis is that it is usually billed as a major health issue for all older women, without noting the fact that it is actually a health issue primarily for White, Asian and Native American women but that Black and Mexican American women are generally much less affected. Selling the fear to *all* women increases the market for calcium and the bone-scanning technology, but the real pressing health needs of older Black, Native American and Mexican American women, as defined by these women, are ignored.

While the fear of osteoporosis had to be sold to women, pervasive cancer phobia is just waiting to be exploited. In total contradiction to the feminist goal of empowering women by providing good health information, seminars promoting women's health centers show that breast cancer education can be presented to women in a way which intentionally plays on the fear factor. Even though it is not clear that mammography actually helps save lives (Whatley and Worcester 1986), a free educational seminar can easily convince women that mammography screening is the one glimmer of hope in the depressing field of breast cancer. Women will buy into the center's screening program, feeling they cannot afford to miss out on this technological hope. Whatley ("Beyond Compliance," this volume) explores how education is used to promote regular mammography and discusses potential problems in the mass marketing of this screening procedure.

CONCLUSION: NEW CHALLENGES FOR THE
WOMEN'S HEALTH MOVEMENT

There is enormous potential for what new women's health centers *could* offer, but the extent to which these serve women will vary greatly from one center to another. Where there is a serious commitment to making services more appropriate to women's needs these centers will be a valuable resource for *some* women. Other centers represent new packaging for some very old problems and are likely to exaggerate the inappropriateness of the medical response to women.

Thus women's health centers create a whole new area of work for the women's health movement, though health activists may feel stymied at first:

> Cooptation poses a dilemma to activists. On the one hand, cooptation insures that some changes will be incorporated into existing institutions. On the other hand, because it reduces discontent, it undermines the impetus for mass action to bring about further change (Ruzek 1980, p. 350).

In spite of the seeming dilemma there are clear directions for action. In each community local groups must monitor the services offered. Where services are valuable to women, local feminists may want to put energy into maximizing what the center could offer. This might mean being involved in feminist education projects or support groups, serving as community representatives, setting up campaigning groups or influencing the center to serve a more diverse group. In many communities feminists will need to criticize the new services and expose the reality behind the existing rhetoric of the marketing information.

The National Women's Health Network's Breast Cancer Campaign (1986) offers an excellent example of how feminists can respond to this latest challenge. The Breast Cancer Campaign will specifically examine the ramifications of slick advertising campaigns urging many women to have breast x-rays at new profit-making centers. The campaign will:

- Conduct a nationwide press campaign to redefine the issue.
- Educate legislators, licensing boards and the public on appropriate standards for mammography clinics.
- Raise the issues of prevention, appropriate testing, and effective treatment for breast cancer in conferences and professional gatherings.
- Press for federal regulations covering breast x-ray equipment.
- Lobby legislators to *require* insurance coverage for mammography screening.
- Meet with professional associations to press for better training on these issues for gynecologists and other health care professionals.

The women's health movement needs to give similar visibility to the controversies and offer possible solutions to problems as new issues, such as osteoporosis screening and the promotion of progesterone through PMS counselling, continue to surface.

Many women committed to the goals of the women's health movement will be taking jobs in the new health centers. It is important that good dialogue exists between feminists choosing to work in the centers and feminists criticizing the centers. Feminist workers will need a source of "reality checks" against which to measure the enthusiasm of hospital administrators and continually to evaluate which services are potentially useful to consumers and which are potentially dangerous. The women's health movement must "be there" for rejuvenating and "supportively-questioning" sisters who are taking on new struggles within the medical system. In exchange, women working within the medical system can help inform our critique so that it accurately addresses the most urgent needs raised by the changing response of the medical system.[3]

There is a danger that white middle-class women, able to afford the services of the highly visible new centers, will be momentarily silenced by the lure of an attractive range of services. But as these centers will do nothing to serve large numbers of women, including those most in need of good health care, it is more crucial than ever that our voices are heard demanding a health care system that meets the real needs of all women.

[3] We thank women working in women's health centers for providing some of the information included in this paper.

REFERENCES

Bills, Sharyn Sweeny. 1984. Women's center brings health promotion, clinical services into full partnership. *Promoting Health*, **5** (6), 1–3.

Boston Women's Health Book Collective. 1984. *The New Our Bodies, Ourselves*. New York: Simon and Schuster.

Bush, Jennifer. 1985. Women's health center, Oak Brook, Ill. *Medicenter Management*, March, 13–14, 18, 21.

Butler, Edith. 1983. The first national conference on Black women's health issues. *WomenWise*, Fall, 2–3.

Center Targets Women's Health Needs. 1984. *Hospitals*, February 16, 58.

Cummings, Steven R., and Black, Dennis. 1986. Should perimenopausal women be screened for osteoporosis? *Annals of Internal Medicine*, **104**, 817–823.

Dallek, Geraldine. 1985. Six myths of American medical care. *Health PAC Bulletin*, **16** (3), 9–15.

Dejanikus, Tacie. 1985. Major drug manufacturer funds osteoporosis education campaign. *The Network News* (National Women's Health Network), May/June, 1–3.

Eagen, Andrea. 1983. The selling of premenstrual syndrome. *Ms*, October, **26**, 28–30.

Folland, Sherman T. 1985. The effects of health care advertising. *Journal of Health Politics, Policy, and Law*, **10** (2), 329–345.

Giges, Nancy. 1986. Calcium market shrugs off study. *Advertising Age*, August 11, **49**, 56.

Harrell, Gilbert D., and Fors, Matthew F. 1985. Marketing ambulatory care to women: a segmentation approach. *Journal of Health Care Marketing*, **5** (2), 19–28.

Jacobs, Gloria. 1986. One-stop health care for women. *Ms*, May, 44–47, 112.

Jensen, Joyce, and Miklovic, Ned. 1986. Consumers cite physicians' interest as most important factor in selection. *Modern Healthcare*, January 17, 48–49.

McGuinn, Sandra. 1982. Center takes women's health beyond maternity. *Booster* (Chicago Lerner Newspaper), May 12, 1.

Ott, Susan. 1986. Should women get screening bone mass measurements? *Annals of Internal Medicine*, **104** (6), 874–876.

Peteros, Karen, and Miller, Fran. 1982. Lesbian health in a straight world. *Second Opinion* (Coalition for the Medical Rights of Women), April, 1–6.

Psychiatric disorders du jour. 1986. *Off Our Backs*, **XVI** (8), 6.

Ruzek, Sheryl Bert. 1980. Medical response to women's health activists: Conflict, accommodation and cooptation. *Research in Sociology of Health Care*, **1**, 335–354.

Rynne, Sally J. 1985. The women's center: a bold strategy. *Health Management Quarterly* Fall-Winter, 12–17.

Sidel, Ruth. 1986. The special plight of older women. In *Women and Children Last*, pp. 157–171. New York: Viking.

Sloane, Ethel. 1985. *Biology of Women*, Second edition. New York: John Wiley.

Smith, Elaine M., Johnson, Susan R., and Guenther, Susan M. 1985. Health care attitudes and experiences during gynecologic care among lesbians and bisexuals. *American Journal of Public Health*, **75** (9), 1085–1087.

Whatley, Mariamne H., and Worcester, Nancy. 1986. The role of technology in the cooption of the women's health movement: the case of osteoporosis and breast cancer screening. Presented at "Women, Health, and Technology Conference," University of Connecticut, October 23, 1986.

Winning with Women's Centers. 1986. *Optimal Health*, May/June, 56–59.

Chapter 8

Beyond Compliance: Towards a Feminist Health Education

Mariamne H. Whatley

One of the major goals of the women's health movement has been to make information about women's bodies and health accessible to all women in demedicalized, clear language. Self-help groups, health collectives, and health-related consciousness-raising groups all demonstrated that a medical expert is not required to tell us what is going on in our own bodies and that we, in fact, have special expertise from which health care professionals might learn. One important point raised in these groups is that a woman can know her own body better than anyone else, including a "trained" person. As she acquires basic knowledge a woman will be able to notice changes in her body and recognize warning signs, so that she can make appropriate lifestyle changes or seek medical (or non-medical) advice. Recognizing this important role for us in our own health care helped us gain more control of our bodies and our health. Numerous publications, seminars and workshops arising from the movement helped demystify both female physiology and the medical system, as well as validating women's own experiences. One result of making information accessible was to enable women to see the relationships between our role as women in this society, our health issues, and our access to quality health care.

The newly-acquired knowledge and power did have an impact, including:

1. Increased awareness among women of the potential role we could play in our own health care.

2. Individual changes in personal health-related behavior.

3. Consumer pressure on health care practitioners to be more responsive to women's health needs, especially in the area of communicating complete information so that the term "informed consent" might have real meaning.

131

4. Pressure from women's health groups and from many women making similar demands causing some basic changes in health care, such as making the one-step biopsy-mastectomy procedure optional rather than automatic.

These changes are positive but perhaps not as impressive as they sound. There have certainly been some changes that have benefited individuals, especially white middle-class women. Within the health care system there also is an awareness of the need at least to *seem* responsive to women's needs. But many of the changes have been merely cosmetic, giving the illusion that women's demands are being responded to. For example, birthing rooms and centers often create a homelike, demedicalized childbirth environment while the medical priorities and who controls the decisions remain the same, and the rate of Cesarean sections continues to climb, from 4% to 20% in the last 15 years (Sheehan 1985).

To anyone studying the market, the sales figures for the various editions of *Our Bodies, Ourselves* have been an indication of the strong interest in women's health information. Recognizing this apparent market a number of writers from outside the movement began producing materials on women's health without necessarily either understanding or dealing with the politics of the issues. Health care facilities also began offering seminars, lectures, and workshops on specific women's health issues, most recently in conjunction with the new women's health centers (discussed in Worcester and Whatley, this volume). But what may seem a positive response to the demands of women's health activists for accessible information is really often nothing more than a use of rhetoric from the women's health movement, while serving a purpose in direct contradiction to the goals of the movement.

An illustration of this point is the annual women's health day, sponsored and organized by a large university hospital. The program consists of a series of lectures and workshops on a wide range of women's health issues, with hospital physicians often serving as speakers. One year I gave the opening address, entitled "Taking Control of our own Health," which presented examples, both contemporary and historical, of ways in which the health care system had taken control away from women and ways in which women had fought and could fight back. In a follow-up workshop the male physician speaker said that he had not heard my talk. He was sure, however, that what I had talked about was taking control of your own health by going to your doctor and doing what he [sic] says.

This example illustrates a key difference between feminist women's health education and education about women's health from the viewpoint of the medical/health care establishment. The goal of the former is to provide complete, accurate information so that women can make truly informed decisions based on our own needs. The latter is often to provide the information that will convince women to make the decision that the health educator has already decided is the correct one.

Unfortunately, the second approach follows one of the common models of health education. The health-related behaviors the educator wants the learners in the program to achieve are decided *first,* so that the health educator, often in conjunction with health care workers, is making decisions about what is best for a given population. The educational program might, at its worst, involve any sort of manipulation deemed necessary to reach that goal. Tactics may include provision of selective information, emphasis on only the positive or negative consequences of a given behavior, ignoring or belittling alternatives, and the use of the scare tactics (popular traditionally in driver-education films which show the goriest of accidents). While lip service may still be paid to the concept of informed decision-making too often only one decision is considered correct.

Clearly, "correct" behaviors or choices vary with class and race. A classic example of this was education around the issue of sterilization. An influential factor was the "120 rule," an unofficial guideline of the American College of Obstetricians and Gynecologists until 1970, which held that before a woman of appropriate race and class could be sterilized, her age multiplied by the number of her children had to equal at least 120 (Clarke 1984). Therefore, a 30-year-old white middle-class woman would need to have four children before being allowed that option, and would be strongly discouraged from sterilization. Since women could not be forbidden to have the surgery, the information presented was likely to be very negative, emphasizing the risks and the most unpleasant details of the surgery, often with accompanying photographs.

On the other hand poor women (especially those on welfare) might have received information pushing them towards sterilization (Clarke 1984). One approach was to present as little information as possible, neglecting, for example, to mention that the procedure is irreversible. One study Clarke cited found that 40% of previously sterilized women thought they could become pregnant again. Another approach was to belittle the effectiveness of the women's current contraceptive and to fail to discuss contraceptive alternatives, so that sterilization might have seemed the only option. Supposedly, sterilization abuse has been eliminated by a number of laws, but it still occurs through more subtle means, such as these misuses of health education. The alarmingly high rates of sterilization among such groups as Native American and Puerto Rican women serve as a reminder that the abuses continue, even though this sterilization may be labeled "voluntary."

We would like to dismiss this example as outdated, but the philosophy underlying such educational abuse still exists. In order to examine the impact the women's health movement has had on health education it is necessary to look at the basic models, issues, and goals involved in the forms of health education found in health care facilities.

PATIENT EDUCATION AND COMPLIANCE

Health education can be broadly defined as "any combination of learning opportunities designed to facilitate adaptations of behavior conducive to health" (Green 1979, p. 160). Within a health care facility the traditional form of health education has been patient education, which basically involves information given to a passive patient (Ruzek 1980). The goal of this approach to education is "to increase patient compliance with professionals' recommendations by providing just enough information to get the patient to do what the professional judges best, but not so much information as to frighten the patient or encourage debate" (Ruzek 1980, p. 247). This model for patient education encourages patient obedience, dependency, and passivity, the traditional signs of a "good patient."

Compliance, the goal of patient education, is defined as "the extent to which an individual's behavior coincides with medical advice" (Haynes 1979, pp. 1–2). Compliance and adherence, terms which can be used interchangeably, could include such actions as taking medicine as prescribed, following a specific diet, doing certain exercises, and having recommended follow-up tests (Haynes 1979). Six basic assumptions that underlie much of the research and discussion about compliance are summarized by DiMatteo and DiNicola (1982, p. 250):

1. Modern medicine is effective so that recommendations made by medical practitioners will benefit the patient.
2. The practitioner is an expert in this area because of command of medical knowledge.
3. Rates of compliance are inadequate.

These first three items are the dominant ones in the drive for compliance, though the ethical considerations in the next three clearly modify the traditional authoritative, practitioner-controlled approach:

4. Clinical recommendations must include negotiated consideration of the patient's beliefs, values and needs.
5. The patient is the expert on the issues in #4.
6. Patients retain both the right and responsibility to determine their medical decisions.

In spite of statements 4–6, health care practitioners are unlikely to relinquish control if they firmly believe both in their knowledge and in the efficacy of medical science. If they have not really questioned whether they know best, it will be hard for them to see patients doing the "wrong" thing. Those who hold strongly with compliance as a goal may view non-compliant patients as irresponsible, ignorant, and guilty. Blaming the victim is a common outcome. One of the themes dominating patient education literature is that patients behave less rationally than providers (Mullen 1980).

Much of the emphasis in the compliance literature is on the factors that can either enhance or interfere with compliance. The "health belief model," which has played a major role in much research about health-related behaviors, is central to many discussions of compliance. Studies suggest that patients are more likely to comply with medical and health recommendations if they perceive the illness as having serious consequences, perceive themselves to be susceptible, and perceive benefits to be gained from compliance (Becker et al. 1979). The educator then has to *convince* the patients of these since the issue is really a matter of perception, not objective fact (Becker 1979). What the patient believes is more important than the objective reality.

The term compliance is certainly at odds with the view of health education as helping individuals make informed health care decisions. Critics of the term suggest it implies "subservience, dependence and unquestioning obedience to authority" (D'Onofrio 1980, p. 271) and is "too authoritarian or too condescending" (Jonsen 1979, p. 119). In this view non-compliant patients may be merely reasserting their rights in the decision-making process.

As discussed above one of the basic assumptions in the drive for compliance is that the practitioner does know best and that compliance is healthy (Ruzek 1980). In a discussion of ethical issues in patient education the point is made that "the practitioner has a duty to believe in the efficacy of his or her own prescriptions, and to attempt to bring about the patient's belief as well" (DiMatteo and DiNicola 1982, p. 251). But it is clear for even a casual observer of medical history that this is not the case. Medical recommendations are simply not always healthy. In recent years we can look at such major pieces of bad advice as the prescription of DES for prevention of miscarriages or insertion of the Dalkon shield as the best IUD. Not only is the research often inadequate in terms of potential risks and side effects but also the most well-intentioned practitioner, due to time constraints, must often rely on readily available literature, rather than on an in-depth study of all the research.

Unfortunately, this literature is usually that presented by the drug companies. Millions of dollars are spent in advertising prescription drugs, so that the physician is inundated with messages about specific products. Even when physicians have more time to read the research literature, they may be reading about research funded by these same companies. The huge marketing campaign that made the Dalkon Shield the IUD of choice was based on poor data from studies conducted by a researcher who had an economic interest in the product (Dowie and Johnston 1977). In cases such as this the advice given to the patient is likely to have a strong bias determined by the information available to the physician.

In addition to the risks from medical intervention and treatments it may be psychologically healthier to be a bad patient. "Model" patients may not do as well (D'Onofrio 1980), probably due to the extreme passivity and dependence this role often entails. They may, for example, accept treatment that is actually inappropriate for their particular needs. This passivity and dependency are symptoms of what Jerrold Greenberg (1985) calls "iatrogenic health education disease," defined as a disease caused by, or its development aided by, health education practices. Symptoms of this disease in a program include coercion and manipulation to get people to behave in healthy ways, as well as use of words such as compliance and adherence. As he and other critics have pointed out, health education can make people sick.

In spite of all the criticism the goal of compliance still dominates health education in medical settings. Many consumer advocates point out that the practitioner's assumption of the right to give orders to the patient is the basis for much criticism of the health care system. But this has been misunderstood and misinterpreted. One author states that "it has been suggested that poor medical outcomes resulting from non-compliance may account for a considerable portion of the general dissatisfaction currently expressed toward the delivery of health care" (Becker 1979, p. 1). This view misses the point that the dissatisfaction arises partially because there is a medical system that uses the term and concept compliance.

SELF-CARE EDUCATION

With the increasing recognition that dependency and passivity may in themselves be unhealthy, educators began to develop the alternative model of self-care education, very similar to the model generated by feminist health groups. In this model goals are derived from "the *learner's* perceived needs and preferences, regardless of whether or not they conform to professional perceptions of the learner's needs" (Levin 1980, p. 208). Control in this model shifts away from the professional to the lay person. This approach can help prevent iatrogenic (physician-induced) illness since it encourages people to look critically at the risks from the health care system itself.

As health care consumers have begun to identify themselves as such, rather than as passive patients caught in the medical machinery, demands for a move from the traditional compliance-oriented model of education have increased. The self-care model therefore provides a welcome alternative. As with much of the response to consumer pressure some changes do occur. Both the patient education and the self-care education approaches exist in many health care facilities, but, in spite of the clear distinctions in focus, the danger is that they often may end up overlapping. What may seem to be self-care education controlled by health care consumers may be directed very strongly by the goals of the health care professionals. The question then is: how far below the surface do these changes actually go? Before attempting to answer this it is necessary to examine the role health education has in economic and marketing terms, since it is often economic pressure that would lead to revisions in the system. The very fact that health care facilities offer educational programs is a sign of the recognition of consumer interest in obtaining health information.

MARKETING THROUGH EDUCATION

Patient education has long been seen as having the very useful dual functions of producing income and encouraging patients to fit into the system (Levin 1980). In the 1970s health education in clinical settings was often justified by its economic benefits such as fewer missed appointments. Now, as health educators become increasingly concerned with issues of professionalism, licensure, and certification, they also may view themselves more as part of the medical team. However they view themselves, they can certainly play an important role in carrying out the wishes of the health care practitioners. In addition, as long as they offer information and health care skills *not* competitive with professional services, they can have some freedom in their programs (Levin 1980). The basic issues around limits of health care education are well summarized in a statement by a State Hospital Association committee quoted by Levin (1980, p. 207):

> Is it counterproductive, from a practical financial standpoint, for hospitals, which derive the greatest part of their resource from inpatient care, to urge courses of action for people which, if followed, may conceivably reduce hospital income?

It is clear then that there are boundaries to health education; encouraging pelvic self-examination at home, for example, could lose good income for practitioners.

However, the selling point is not simply that health education may make work easier for practitioners (so long as it does not tread on certain medical turf). An important factor now is that health education can be used as a marketing strategy very effectively. As hospitals, HMOs, clinics, and women's health centers compete for customers, educational programs become an important form of advertising. The marketability of women's health education has been well demonstrated by the popularity of publications, seminars, and classes in this area. The women's health movement stressed education as a need and a goal and the women's health centers, having seen the interest, also put emphasis there. Marketing strategies for these centers emphasize the use of educational programs to attract women to use their facilities (Worcester and Whatley, this volume).

FWS-F

POTENTIAL PITFALLS FOR THE NEW WOMEN'S HEALTH EDUCATION

For health education to play a successful role in the promotion of women's health centers many of the obvious problems associated with patient education must be avoided. Given the impact of the women's health movement in terms of increasing women's awareness of our rights in the health care system, it would be much harder for a practitioner or educator to get by with an authoritative, paternalistic approach. It has been suggested that health educators and practitioners should develop the characteristics of a good persuader, such as enthusiasm, confidence, interest, and trustworthiness (DiMatteo and DiNicola 1982, p. 183). More compliance was shown in health care programs if, among other factors, health care professionals showed care, warmth and concern in interactions (Feldman 1985). The women's health movement has also called for real caring and concern in practitioners. Unfortunately, these can be simulated both to appear to meet this need and to get better compliance. If educators and practitioners are truly recognizing the need for an active, informed role in health care decision-making for the consumer, then there could be an excellent feminist educational program. But it is also possible to use the form and not the principles of the women's health movement to suit the needs of the clinical facility.

One of the important developments to arise from the women's health movement was the development of lay-controlled self-help groups. These relied on expertise based on experience rather than on professional credentials (Ruzek 1980). They played a major role in helping women gain control of our health and assert our rights in the health care system. Some of these groups formed around a specific shared experience, such as surviving rape or having breast cancer, while others had a broader focus such as the politics of health. Besides validating women's experiences and perceptions they explored alternatives in health care. These groups often then produced publications or did community education which made the information they had generated accessible to other women. Health issues were placed in the context of the role of women in society and the impact they could have on women's lives. Often these groups took the logical next steps of consumer activism and political action. Many women developed leadership and organizational skills through involvement in such groups.

Women's health centers can do a great service to the community by keeping lists of all the available self-help groups and similar resources. Appropriate referrals to such diverse groups as those for battered women, survivors of incest, women with eating disorders, women who have breast cancer, and women who weight train can be an important function. But it is necessary to keep in mind that these groups must be free of pressures from the health care system. Invitations to use center space are fine as long as that does not entail any obligation or dependency. The relationship of the health care or health education professional to these groups should be that primarily of a resource person (Ruzek 1980). They can also contribute by making referrals to appropriate groups. The potential danger that exists is the temptation for professionals to manage these groups (Levin 1980). For professionals to organize the group in any way would be subverting the purpose of self-help and the major benefits to be gained from lay control would be lost.

For health education programs to prove their value in clinical settings they must do more than attract people to the facility. Women's health centers tend to focus on several specific women's health issues, some of which are associated with fairly expensive technologies. Unfortunately, for commercial reasons, a health education program might push women into using these technologies, whether appropriate or not for their needs. The next section explores an area in which there could potentially be health education abuse, particularly within women's health centers.

BREAST CANCER AND MAMMOGRAPHY

The kind of manipulative health education that can be done is illustrated by looking at education relating to breast cancer. A goal of this education is to convince women to have mammography, a major offering of women's health clinics. While mammography shows great potential as both a diagnostic and screening tool there are still many problems associated with it (Whatley and Worcester 1986). Included among these is the necessity for highly-trained technicians and radiologists, becoming ever harder to find as centers offering mammography multiply. Also as the technology becomes more refined it will be necessary to have the most up-to-date equipment, the cost of which must then be justified by increasing use. In addition, what may be ignored in the educational program on the benefits of mammography are the higher number both of false negatives, resulting in an unwarranted sense of security, and of false positives, resulting in unnecessary biopsies and sometimes even mastectomies. At this point the recommendations for who should use mammography at what age and at what intervals are still being debated (Hall 1986; Skrabanek 1985).

One way of examining the health education issues around mammography is to look at the health belief model and compliance. Becker (1979) discusses a study by Kegeles (1969) on women's participation in a cervical cancer screening program. Women were more "compliant" if they believed the test could detect cancer, would reveal illness before clinical symptoms, and would lead to a more favorable prognosis. In general in this model, individuals must see themselves as at risk and be convinced that the recommended procedure might work. These criteria can be applied to breast cancer:

1. *Personal susceptibility*. Breast cancer is very prevalent in the United States; one out of eleven women will develop breast cancer. In addition most women can be found to have some risk factors. For example many have a close female relative who had breast cancer. An unethical educator might neglect to point out that this risk only holds if the relative developed the cancer *premenopausally*. Women who gave birth to their first child before age 18 are at less risk than those whose first child is born after age 35; having no children is a risk, as is giving birth after age 30. The childbearing patterns of many of the women who can afford mammography therefore put them at risk. Certain crucial information might be left out, such as that many women with high-risk factors never get breast cancer or that there are risks that can be reduced, such as lowering intake of fat in the diet, especially animal fats, and reducing exposure to radiation, such as from mammography.

2. *Severity of disease*. The severity of breast cancer is probably firmly implanted in most women's minds without need for further education.

3. *Effectiveness of screening*. The information about mammography generally suggests that it can detect cancer before the mass can be palpated. The information about false negatives and false positives may not be presented.

4. *Improved prognosis*. The selling point of the whole procedure is that early detection will lead to a better prognosis. This is a question that is very much debated. Early detection may lead only to an *apparent* longer survival rate, due simply to identifying the cancer earlier (Skrabanek 1985). In order to convince people of the value of the procedure educators must ignore the possibility that early detection makes no difference.

The case with cervical cancer screening is more clear cut than with breast cancer, but the same principles of what would guarantee "compliance" may hold very well. With breast cancer screening, this may require leaving out some pieces of information and not involving the client in a complex medical debate, perhaps "for her own good."

In the same educational setting as she receives this information, a women can have a "geography" lesson on her breasts. While this could be very useful since many women are insecure about breast self-examination (never being sure of exactly what they are feeling) it could also be used as an opportunity to encourage mammography. This procedure would give assurance as to what each lump or bump really is. Education can be used to increase fear and create insecurity about a woman's understanding of her own body. The answer is the use of a readily available medical technology, in this case mammography. Having a baseline mammogram is seen as a preventive measure, when, in fact, at best it is an early detection measure.

With the emphasis on prevention in the women's health movement, women might easily be encouraged to have this done. Besides possibly pushing women to use an expensive technology that may not benefit them, this health education approach can lead to more dependence on the health care system and medical technology while decreasing options for personal control.

THE CURRENT STATE OF WOMEN'S HEALTH EDUCATION

Currently much of the education around women's health issues is a response to the demands of the women's health movement on the surface only. It is clear that women's health books sell well, seminars on these topics are crowded, as are university courses on women's health. Directors of health care facilities have identified educational programs as a major way of competing with each other for the limited healthy, middle-class clientele. These programs can also serve to encourage use of specific medical services, such as mammography and bone density measurement. Health education can also be used to create new markets; premenstrual syndrome clinics are now opening in many cities.

All of these educational programs are packaged in a way that emphasizes concern, caring and trustworthiness. (It may truly be there in many cases, but that is not the point.) The message is that all the information will be presented so that the consumer can make an informed decision. But in many cases the information is incomplete or biased. The health education models that have compliance as a goal still dominate education in a clinical setting. It may be hard for health educators to keep in mind some basic ethical issues at the same time that they are fighting to justify their existence in commercial terms to the managers of the facility.

TOWARDS A FEMINIST HEALTH EDUCATION

What would constitute a true feminist health education? It is sometimes hard to imagine changes in a system that seems so established, but feminist input would certainly make health education very different. It is interesting to compare this issue to discussions of what would constitute feminist science, a concept many people have trouble accepting. Envisioning the possibility for a feminist science, Fee (1983) used the example of the changes in occupational health research in Italian factories. Before 1969 management identified a problem and hired experts to investigate the issue. Using "rigorously objective" procedures they gathered quantifiable information, statistically manipulated the data, and tested their hypotheses. In 1969 the approach was radically changed with the advent of direct democracy involving workers' committees. Workers collectively produced the information necessary and collectively generated their hypotheses. Following that, the specialists discussed their research ideas with the workers' assemblies, seeing "their 'objective' expertise measured against the 'subjective' experience of the workers. The mutual validation of data took place by testing it in terms of the workers' experience of reality and not simply by statistical methods" (Fee, 1983, p. 24).

The pre-1969 approach is similar to the approach to patient education discussed earlier. Experts make decisions, based on their "objective" and scientific knowledge, on what is best for those they are supposed to help. The post-1969 approach is very similar to what feminists have been pushing for in the health care system in the United States. The "experts" must recognize and validate the "subjective" experience of women; these experts can provide their "objective" expertise as resource people. Imposition of their scientific definitions of health and health problems on passive clients/patients is unacceptable.

Feminist health education would involve integrating the basic philosophies and goals of the women's health movement. There are a number of points that should be considered, including:

1. Motivating factors for the development of health education programs would not be commercial considerations for health care providers, publishers, or manufacturers. As Levin (1980, p. 214) suggests, it is important to "distinguish between programs stimulated by needs *of* patients and those stimulated by needs *for* patients."

2. Health education priorities would be determined by real health needs of different groups of women as determined by those women. The major health education programs would not be aimed at fine-tuning the health of already very healthy women, but at first pushing for minimal standards of health for all women.

3. Information would take into account a diversity of experiences, health needs, and resources. Presenting the *best* solution in medical terms ignores the simple fact that it is not best for all women. For example an educator may recommend the perfect prenatal diet without paying attention to religious restrictions, cultural preferences, and lack of money.

4. Information provided would be truly accessible to all women. That would include translation into appropriate languages, though it is important to realize that translating Anglo health education materials into Spanish does not constitute Hispanic health education. The information would be available in many forms, depending on the needs of the population served. These might include the more predictable approaches of using pamphlets, videotapes, audiotapes, and computer software, but also would explore other options such as street theater, clowns and traditional storytelling.

5. Information would be complete, without selecting only that which suits the educator's needs. Protecting women from medical complexities and controversies "for their own good" would not be acceptable.

6. The educator would *never* predetermine a set of behaviors or outcomes that women should follow. A combination of the woman's expertise about her own needs and options with the health expertise of the educator would be used to generate appropriate solutions.

7. Women drawn from the community would serve on advisory boards to ensure that programs were relevant to the lives of real women, not just to a targeted market segment.

8. Health educators would help stimulate formation of self-help groups, make referrals to them, act as resources, and otherwise leave them alone.

9. The health educator would continue to learn from the population served.

All of this may seem idealistic and impossible given commercial constraints and political realities. But health educators who want to do true women's health education must keep these goals in mind, aiming for them even if we sometimes fall short.

REFERENCES

Becker, M. H. 1979. Understanding patient compliance: The contributions of attitudes and other psychosocial factors. In S. J. Cohen (ed.), *New Directions in Patient Compliance*, pp. 1–31. Lexington, MA: Lexington Books.

Becker, M. H., Maiman, L. A., Kirscht, J. P., Haefner, D. P., Drachman, R. H., and Taylor, D. W. 1979. Patient perceptions and compliance: Recent studies of the health belief model. In R. B. Haynes, D. W. Taylor and D. L. Sackett (eds), *Compliance in Health Care*, pp. 78–109. Baltimore: The Johns Hopkins University Press.

Clarke, A. 1984. Subtle forms of sterilization abuse. In R. Arditti, R. D. Klein and S. Minden (eds), *Test-tube Women: What Future for Motherhood?* pp. 188–212. London: Pandora Press.

DiMatteo, M. R., and DiNicola, D. D. 1982. *Achieving Patient Compliance: The Psychology of the Medical Practitioner's Role*. New York: Pergamon Press.

D'Onofrio, C. N. 1980. Patient compliance and patient education: Some fundamental issues. In W. D. Squyres (ed.), *Patient Education: An Inquiry into the State of the Art*, pp. 271–279. New York: Springer Publishing.

Dowie, M., and Johnston, T. 1977. A case of corporate malpractice and the Dalkon Shield. In C. Dreifus (ed.), *Seizing our Bodies: The Politics of Women's Health*, pp. 86–104. New York: Vintage Books.

Fee, E. 1983. Women's nature and scientific objectivity. In M. Lowe and R. Hubbard (eds), *Woman's Nature: Rationalizations of Inequality*, pp. 9–27. New York: Pergamon Press.

Feldman, R. H. L. 1985. The assessment and enhancement of health compliance in the workplace. In G. S. Everly, Jr. and R. H. L. Feldman (eds), *Occupational Health Promotion: Health Behavior in the Workplace*, pp. 33–46. New York: John Wiley and Sons.

Green, L. W. 1979. Educational strategies to improve compliance with therapeutic and preventive regimens: The recent evidence. In R. B. Haynes, D. W. Taylor and D. L. Sackett (eds), *Compliance in Health Care*, pp. 157–173. Baltimore: The Johns Hopkins University Press.

Greenberg, J. S. 1985. Iatrogenic health education disease. *Health Education*, **16** (5), 4–6.

Hall, Ferris M. 1986. Screening mammography-potential problems on the horizon. *The New England Journal of Medicine*, **314** (1), 53–55.

Haynes, R. B. 1979. Introduction. In R. B. Haynes, D. W. Taylor and D. L. Sackett (eds), *Compliance in Health Care,* pp. 1–7. Baltimore: The Johns Hopkins University Press.

Jonsen, A. R. 1979. Ethical issues in compliance. In R. B. Haynes, D. W. Taylor and D. L. Sackett (eds), *Compliance in Health Care,* pp. 113–120. Baltimore: The Johns Hopkins University Press.

Kegeles, S. S. 1969. A field experiment attempt to change beliefs and behavior of women in an urban ghetto. *Journal of Health and Social Behavior,* **10,** 115–124.

Levin, L. S. 1980. Patient education and self-care: How do they differ? In W. D. Squyres (ed.), *Patient Education: An Inquiry into the State of the Art,* pp. 205–216. New York: Springer Publishing.

Mullen, P. D. 1980. The (already) activated patient: An alternative to medicocentrism. In W. D. Squyres (ed.), *Patient Education: An Inquiry into the State of the Art,* pp. 281–298. New York: Springer Publishing.

Ruzek, S. B. 1980. Women's self-help programs. In W. D. Squyres (ed.), *Patient Education: An Inquiry into the State of the Art,* pp. 247–270. New York: Springer Publishing.

Sheehan, K. H. 1985, July/August. Abnormal labor: Cesareans in the U.S. *The Network News* (National Women's Health Network), pp. 1, 3.

Skrabanek, P. 1985, August 10. False premises and false promises of breast cancer screening. *The Lancet,* 8450, pp. 316–319.

Whatley, M. H., and Worcester, N. 1986. The role of technology in the cooption of the women's health movement: The case of osteoporosis and breast cancer screening. Presented at "Women, Health, and Technology Conference," University of Connecticut, October 23, 1986.

4
Conclusion

The Need for Women and Feminism to Overcome Resistance in Science and Health Care

Sue V. Rosser

Within the last two decades women have made significant strides in entering professions in science and health care. Altekruse and McDermott demonstrate the tremendous increase from 6% in 1960 to 33% by 1985 of first-year female medical students. Kronenfeld's data illustrate the marked increase in women in public health. Gero has shown that large numbers of women are present in archeology, although they are not dispersed equally within the subspecialties within the fields. Even within the physical sciences Vetter's data document an increase in the actual numbers of women, particularly within the last decade.

Unfortunately, the data in the chapters by these same individuals also demonstrate that very few of these women have reached high-level decision-making positions in their profession. This undoubtedly has been one of the factors contributing to the resistances to feminism described by the other authors in the volume. Absence of women on editorial boards may explain Bleier's finding that editorial policies of the major scientific journals favor theories in the neurosciences that support biological differences between males and females as justification for social inequalities. My chapter indicates that despite increasing numbers women in science may still be reluctant or uninterested in presenting feminist topics at major scientific meetings. The work of Worcester and Whatley suggests that feminist ideas, when accepted, may be distorted and twisted by traditional health care practitioners so that they no longer benefit women.

Understanding the extent to which these resistances of science and health care to women and feminism have biased theory and practice, many feminists have called for the rejection of science. Some feminists conclude that current science and health care must be rejected because they are based upon a masculine domination of both nature and women. The work of Keller (1985) and Merchant (1979) documents that at the birth of modern science it was the mechanistic approach, which implied male distance from and superiority over both women and nature, which became dominant compared with other approaches which were more holistic and egalitarian towards women and nature.

Given the technological complexity of our modern society and some of the established benefits of medicine it seems impractical to see the rejection of science as a solution. Rejection of science and a refusal of feminists to become scientists would lead to further distance and resistance between women and science. Since our society *is* scientific and technological, this rejection would lead women to being further outside the mainstream of our society. Without any feminists in science or health care, the theory and practice would be likely to show no accommodation to a feminist critique.

A more realistic solution would be provided by having more women in science and more feminists interested in and trained as scientists and health care practitioners.

Two areas on the leading edge of modern science and health care make it quite clear exactly how much we need women in decision-making positions in science. These areas, the first a combination of basic science and health care, the second a combination of basic science and public policy, also focus why feminists and scientists must lower their resistance and listen to the perspectives and information each can give to the other.

1. Reproductive technologies

Reproductive technologies include the full range of biomedical/technical interferences during the processes of procreation, whether aimed at producing a child or preventing/terminating pregnancy. Usually the newer technologies refer to artificial reproductive techniques such as *in vitro* fertilization, artificial insemination, surrogate mothers, sex pre-selection, and cloning accomplished by *in vitro* methods. Although most of the techniques are applied to women and some are desperately sought after by women, they have been developed, administered and regulated almost exclusively by men. Some of the language which the men used to describe the women undergoing the techniques is frightening. Their plans for future uses of these techniques are horrifying:

> There is (. . .) the use of the "genius sperm bank" a laboratory in Escondido, in California, which stores samples of sperm obtained from highly intelligent men, including some Nobel Prize Winners (. . .) the founder of the sperm bank, the millionaire Robert Graham, intends to inseminate specially selected women with a view to contributing to an improvement in mankind's Genetic Standards.

Nakamura says that studies at the Melbourne Australian Facility have revealed the possibility of men conceiving a child. "They discovered that from a physiological point of view it is perfectly possible for a man to carry an *in vitro* inseminated ovum but the commissions in charge of designating funds have not accepted the programme, which has been shelved until further notice" (Gomez Dos Reis 1987, p. 205).

In addition the failure rates for some of the technologies such as IVF are extremely high, although most of the companies report their statistics in ways that mislead the women seeking the procedure.

Of the 54 clinics responding to our questionnaire, half have never sent a woman home with a baby. These zero success clinics have been in business from one month to three years and have treated more than 600 women (Corea and Ince, in press, p. 219).

The undisputed leader in IVF deliveries is Eastern Virginia Medical School, where Drs. Howard and Georgeanna Jones also obtained the first IVF pregnancy in the U.S. three years ago. They now have 100 babies delivered to 89 mothers. As noted, only a handful of other clinics reported achieving more than five births in their clinics' histories (Corea and Ince, in press, p. 221).

Responding to pressure from IVF colleagues, "The Code of the West [the rule] now is that you don't report chemical pregnancies," Dr. Holman told us. "But I think you have to be very careful. If you have a new program that's done 50–60 attempts and the only thing they've got is a couple of chemical pregnancies, it's very easy for them to say, 'We've had two pregnancies,' and not be too specific. It's not that they're deceiving anyone but it's really not exactly the same thing" (Corea and Ince, in press, p. 227).

I say to the patients, "For every 100 people that come in the room, at least 85 go home without a baby, even after doing everything right."

This implies a live birth rate of approximately 15%, yet her clinic's questionnaire reported a less than 3% live birth rate. Asked how she came up with her 15% figure, she said: "Taking an average of 15%. But I think it's 10–20% worldwide" (Corea and Ince, in press, p. 229).

We desperately need more women scientists who are qualified to work with these techniques, evaluate grant proposals for funding the technologies, and serve on the governing boards of hospitals, laboratories and clinics where these technologies are being used. I would like to see the entire direction that this research is taking changed. I think that women scientists in decision-making positions to control this research would be likely to have that effect. At minimum, women in these positions would change the current situation of male-only groups and governing boards making decisions about techniques that will be practiced on only women's bodies.

2. Nuclear research

Since the 1940s both men and women have been alternately amazed and frightened by the positive potential and threat of destruction generated by research in nuclear physics. The development of nuclear power plants in the 1960s and 1970s further reinforced the double-edged nature of nuclear power. The tremendous resourse for providing cheap power was very attractive; disposal of waste and the inevitability of an eventual plant accident were horrifying.

More recently the escalating militarism and renewed threats of militarism of the 1980s have led individuals to become concerned again about the effects of nuclear waste and destruction on people and the environment. The Chernobyl accident was a graphic realization of these fears. People actually saw the destroyed landscape around the plant and heard the statistics of death, cancer, and deformity for the accident victims. Women's groups in Europe in the movement known as ecofeminism have taken the lead in making explicit the connection between the potential destruction of the environment and women's bodies by uncontrolled use of science and technology. The women of the Feminist Women's Health Centre in Frankfurt, Germany made the following statements on May 24, 1986 at the Romer anti-nuclear demonstration, a month after the Chernobyl disaster.

> Almost everyone in this country felt the whiff of death in these longed for early spring days. We were and still are torn by conflicting feelings: rage, depression and hopelessness before the creeping, invisible destruction potential of nuclear contamination — together with and additional to all the other problems we have anyway: ecological, economic, mental and health. The urge to give up, to resign oneself will constantly assail us — but being resigned also means anticipating death . . . .

> For over two thousand years patriarchy has been exploiting nature: earth, plants, animals and people are subjugated, violated and destroyed. As a refinement and historical further development of the methods this destruction is now being consummated in a totally desensualized and invisible way by nuclear contamination . . . .

> Total dismantling of all life-scorning and life-destroying technologies and machinery is the only solution . . . .

We women in the United States must become active in decision-making positions in the governmental and scientific hierarchy. Only when we lower the barriers between the science and health care systems and feminism can we hope to change those systems to include the needs of women. Only as women who are feminists and scientists can we attempt to develop a science and health care system that will benefit all human beings, including women and children. If women do not become involved in science and its public policies we become not only a gender at risk, but part of a species at risk.

REFERENCES

Corea, G., and Ince, S. Report of a survey of IVF clinics in the USA. *Made to Order: The Myth of Reproductive and Genetic Progress*, P. Spallone and D. L. Steinberg (eds), New York: Pergamon Press. *In press.*

Feminist Women's Health Centre, Frankfurt. Chernobyl and After. *Made to Order: The Myth of Reproductive and Genetic Progress*, P. Spallone and D. L. Steinberg (eds), New York: Pergamon Press. *In press.*

Gomez Dos Reis, A. R. IVF in Brazil: the story told by the newspapers. *Made to Order: The Myth of Reproductive and Genetic Progress*, P. Spallone and D. L. Steinberg (eds), New York: Pergamon Press. *In press.*

Keller, E. F. 1985. *Reflections on Gender, and Science.* New Haven: Yale University Press.

Merchant, C. 1979. *The Death of Nature: Women, Ecology and the Scientific Revolution.* New York: Harper and Row.

About the Editor and Contributors

THE EDITOR

Sue V. Rosser is the Director of Women's Studies at the University of South Carolina at Columbia. She also holds an appointment as Associate Professor of Preventive Medicine and Community Health in the USC Medical School. Formerly she was Chair of the Division of Theoretical and Natural Sciences and Coordinator of Women's Studies at Mary Baldwin College. She received her Ph.D. degree in Zoology in 1973 from the University of Wisconsin-Madison and while a post-doctoral fellow began teaching in the women's studies program at the University of Wisconsin during the first year of its existence in 1976. Since then she has taught courses in both biology and women's studies programs at the University of Wisconsin-Madison and Mary Baldwin College. She is the author of several publications dealing with the theoretical and applied problems of women and science, and the book *Teaching About Science and Health from a Feminist Perspective: A Practical Guide*, published by Pergamon Press. As a consultant for the Wellesley Center for Research on Women she has worked with faculty at several institutions that are attempting to include the new scholarship on women in the science curriculum.

THE CONTRIBUTORS

Joan M. Altekruse, M.D., M.P.H., Dr.P.H., Professor and Chair of the Department of Preventive Medicine at the University of South Carolina School of Medicine, is an active participant in academic and community medicine, serving currently as President of the American Teachers of Preventive Medicine, and recently as President of the South Carolina Affiliate of the American Heart Association. She works with local and national groups concerned with the advancement of women in higher education and in medicine. Her special interests in research, policy setting, and health care delivery focus on the area of maternal and child health.

153

Ruth Bleier was trained as a physician and practiced medicine for several years before becoming a neuroanatomist. She is a professor in the Department of Neurophysiology and the Women's Studies Program at the University of Wisconsin-Madison. She uses light and electron microscopes to study the structure and organization of the part of the brain known as the hypothalamus. Since the early 1970s she has been engaged in the feminist critical analysis of the assumptions and methods of the natural sciences in their millenial project of constructing gender, gender differences, and the concept of Woman. She has written one book on this subject, *Science and Gender: A Critique of Biology and its Theories on Women*, and edited another, *Feminist Approaches to Science*, both published by Pergamon Press.

Joan Gero is an Assistant Professor of anthropology at the University of South Carolina with research interests in the pre-Incaic societies of Peru. She has conducted archeological field research in England, Labrador, Massachusetts, South Carolina and Rhode Island in addition to Peru, and has edited a volume (together with D. Lacy and M. Blakey) entitled *The Socio-politics of Archeology*. She is currently carrying out field research in the Callejon de Huaylas region of highland Peru and is co-editing a Blackwells Publication volume (with M. Conkey) called *Women's Production in Prehistory*.

Jennie J. Kronenfeld is a professor in the Department of Health Administration, School of Public Health at the University of South Carolina. Her doctorate is in sociology from Brown University. She has published widely in sociological, public health and medical journals and has published books on the health care delivery system, health care policy and changes in sex roles..

Suzanne W. McDermott, M.S.N., M.S.P.H., is currently involved in research projects related to the health care of handicapped children and other groups (e.g., Migrant Farm Workers) receiving inadequate health care services. She has worked in health planning on a local and regional level and has been trained as a Nurse Practitioner for Handicapped Children and Adults. As Research Coordinator for the Department of Preventive Medicine at the University of South Carolina School of Medicine, and Vice-president of the Association for Retarded Citizens of South Carolina, she is interested in policy development and medical research.

Betty M. Vetter is the Executive Director of the Commission on Professionals in Science and Technology, formerly known as the Scientific Manpower Commission. Since the Commission is a participating organization of the American Association for the Advancement of Science, Betty Vetter collects and analyzes statistical data on scientific professionals employed in business, government, and academia.

Mariamne H. Whatley is a biologist who directs the Health Education Program at the University of Wisconsin-Madison and teaches women's biology and health in the Women's Studies Program. Her work involves a feminist critique and transformation of the ways health and sexuality are taught.

Nancy Worcester is a lecturer in the Women's Studies Program, University of Wisconsin-Madison and is on the National Women's Health Network Board. She received her Ph.D. (Nutrition) from the University of London. Nancy has been active in the women's health movement in both England and the United States, was a founding member of the London-based Women's Health Information Center collective, and has led/organized health study tours to China, Cuba, Grenada and Nicaragua.

Index

157

THE ATHENE SERIES
An International Collection of Feminist Books
General Editors: Gloria Bowles, Renate Klein and Janice Raymond
Consulting Editor: Dale Spender